for Doreen,

Merry Christmas 2000

Love,

Jackie

S0-DTA-770

ALL THE WORLD
WAS HIS STAGE

ALL THE WORLD
WAS HIS STAGE

DAVID BROWN
Memories & Mementos

mosaic press

Canadian Cataloguing in Publication Data

Brown, David, 1936 Aug. 9-1999
    David Brown: memories & mementos

Includes bibliographical references.
ISBN 0-88962-750-9

1. Brown, David, 1936 Aug. 9-1999. 2 . Actors – Canada –
Biography. I. Title.

PN2308.B76A3 2000   792'.028'092   C00-932349-X

No part of this book may be reproduced or transmitted in any form, by any
means, electronic or mechanical, including photocopying and recording information storage and retrieval systems, without permission in writing from
the publisher, except by a reviewer who may quote brief passages in a review.

Published by MOSAIC PRESS, P.O. Box 1032, Oakville, Ontario, L6J 5E9,
Canada. Offices and warehouse at 1252 Speers Road, Units #1&2, Oakville,
Ontario, L6L 5N9, Canada and Mosaic Press, 4500 Witmer Industrial Estates,
PMB 145, Niagara Falls, NY 14305-1386

Mosaic Press acknowledges the assistance of the Canada Council and the
Department of Canadian Heritage, Government of Canada for their support of
our publishing programme.

© Copyright 2000, The Authors

MOSAIC PRESS, in Canada:
1252 Speers Road, Units #1 & 2,
Oakville, Ontario, L6L 5N9
Phone / Fax: 905-825-2130
ORDERS:
mosaicpress@on.aibn.com
EDITORIAL:
cp507@freenet.toronto.on.ca

MOSAIC PRESS, in the USA:
4500 Witmer Industrial Estates
PMB 145, Niagara Falls,
NY 14305-1386 Tel:1-800-387-8992
ORDERS:
mosaicpress@on.aibn.com
EDITORIAL:
cp507@freenet.toronto.on.ca

Le Conseil des Arts | The Canada Council
du Canada | for the Arts

DAVID BROWN

Actor, lawyer, bridge player, friend.

Born in Halifax, August 9, 1936.

Died in Edmonton, June 28, 1999 of a cerebral aneurism aged 62.

TABLE OF CONTENTS

PREFACE

First of all, I want to thank Paul Break for putting this whole book together for me, all of the family, and for a very wide circle of friends.

Paul suggested I write a preface explaining why I wanted this book published in the first place. As you read through *All the World Was His Stage*, you will know why I felt compelled to preserve his writings.

I always felt a little sad that David left no children on this earth. The world would have been a better place with more David's in it. Perhaps there would not have been the same loving energies he gave so unselfishly to his friends and family, if we had to share him with a wife and children. Who knows?

David's short stories were worthy of publication, only it just never happened. This was a motivation for me to make sure his writings did not end up stored away in a box, never to be shared, and eventually destroyed. David was the one with the talent – a better writer and cook than I – yet I was the one who ended up the cookbook author, which had far more to do with luck than talent. But no one was more supportive and prouder of my accomplishments than my younger brother. The dedication in my last book, *Low Fat Beef* was 'to David Brown- Brother and Friend'. At the memorial service held for David in Edmonton, my friend Margie McCaffrey sang 'You Are the Wind Beneath my Wings'. David was indeed my 'hero' and 'the wind beneath my wings'.

– Jackie Eddy Caithness

INTRODUCTION

Everybody who ever met David Brown knew he was a born storyteller. Many of us didn't also know he was a born storywriter.

David wrote like he talked and acted: dramatically introduce the attention-grabbing story line; develop it in a series of theatrical 'scenes' decorated with entertaining flourishes and thoughtful observations; and conclude with a perfect wrap-up – sometimes sentimental, usually hilarious, never maudlin, and always satisfying.

Brevity was not one of David's long suits: he gave each story, memoir and letter the length and breadth of scene-setting and detailed character development they deserved in the telling, with the result that David's Complete Collected Works would far exceed two large volumes.

This collection presents a sampler of David's writings, and includes two Travel Diaries, a number of Short Stories, and it concludes with Appreciations of David by some of his close friends and colleagues.

The volume concludes with Sandra Gwyn's inspiring remembrance of David Brown which she read at David's Memorial Service in Toronto in late July 1999. Sandra's remembrance concluded with these words:

"David left us too young and too soon, yet he enhanced all of our lives, just as he lit up the stage at Dalhousie so long ago. And he will continue to do so, from here to eternity – for love is stronger than death."

Sandra Gwyn died of cancer on May 26,2000, a few days after being presented personally with the Order of Canada by Governor-General Adrienne Clarkson. David Brown would have been thrilled. 'Think of the good times that they're having while they wait for the rest of us.'

– *Paul Break*

DIARIES

BICYCLE TRIP THROUGH FRANCE, 1959

*In July – September of 1959, David celebrated his comple-
tion of Law School and his 23rd birthday with his own
unique European Grand Tour: a bicycle tour through
France; then a month of studying French in Grenoble; and
concluding with a spectacular three week tour of Italy.*

July 26: North Finchley–Newhaven–Dieppe

Crossed the channel to Dieppe, through immigration and customs, then direct to a sidewalk café, most gorgeous *chocolat et croissants – c'est merveilleux*. Up the Rue des Canadiens and though magnificent countryside on straight, well-paved roads with Km. Stones to keep you company and clover to intoxicate you.

Had my first accident; i.e. falling off the bike into an unusually comfortable ditch, rendering two gears useless. A man in a bicycle shop fixed it for 100ff. Had a gorgeous meal at an outdoor café immediately under Rouen Cathedral, practicing my few words of French at every opportunity, then pressed on to a youth hostel in Évreux, brand-new place, ultra modern and very good (150f), but I couldn't shit because I got hysterical in the john which is merely two footrests and a hole! Imagine building brand-new bathrooms like that! Also the showers were icy cold!

July 28: Évreux–Dreux–Chartres

Up at 5:30 a.m. and did 77k of very subtle up-hill cycling against the wind. Several times we were applauded by French peasants, who perhaps mistook us for the romantic adventure–Tour de France.

You can see Chartres Cathedral for about 10 miles before you reach it, and a most incredible place it was. I spent hours just spellbound with the medieval atmosphere; and lay on the floor to take a picture, and held up a tour. Later, we overheard the tour leader telling her friend about the incredible German youth lying on the floor taking pictures, and her friend said that a sense of humour was needed for their job.

Chartres has atmosphere up the ass, with narrow, winding streets and the river cutting through and bridges cutting over. Houses ancient, all crooked and in pastel colours in the setting sun with the Cathedral and spires and buttresses as background and music and laughter from the houses and the cafes – like a dream to me. Ate two rum babas which I couldn't resist, then back to the auberge to make tea –quite a healthy atmosphere, but oh! those bathrooms. At times like this, I would prefer a colostomy.

July 29: Chartres–Bonneval–Châteaudun

Two minutes after we started cycling, so did the rain. We looked like two generals in our war–surplus 2nd hand rain capes (which double as ground sheets). With our plans to get to Blois shattered, we took a diversion to the little fortified town of Bonneval, and thank god we did – I shall never forget it! We had our bread, wine, cheese and ham right on the moat by the archway to the village, through which we could see a large cathedral with green windows, people punting on the moat and some women washing clothes there. The sun came out for an hour – marvelous indeed.

With very strong headwinds, but sunny and warm, we continued to Châteaudun, past my very first French chateau in the Loire valley, then on to the Auberge, very tired. The Auberge is filthy, but I like the atmosphere and people. After a walk through town, we had a superb meal, with wine, soup, etc. – oh God, I feel so good after a French dinner, I cycle off a few pounds and put on twice as many when I eat.

July 30: Châteaudun–Beaugency –Chambord–Blois

Good cycling today with favourable conditions. The countryside has changed from fields of hay and vast prairies to more forested parts, and fields of corn and grapes, not ripe enough to filch, worse luck. Beaugency extremely pretty with a large abbey and interesting bridge, between which I had my favourite chocolate and croissants.

We approached Chambord through miles of straight avenue lined on both sides with very tall trees. Chambord Château was a joy to behold, with its delicate and intricate turrets and chimneys surrounded by a moat, where we ate our truly elegant lunch – vintage white wine, bread and paté, yogurt, laughing cow cheese, eggs, chocolate and croissants. Mmmm, the sun blazed down and I was intoxicated completely.

On to Blois, complete with château, bridge, cathedrals, cafés, streets that wind and turn, fascinating every inch of the way. We didn't go in the château, but looked though all the windows, and climbed the elegant staircase built by one of the Kings so he could ride up into the château on his horse.

The Auberge is in the countryside and suprisingly clean, due to a regimental housemother. The W.C. is the same as always, only you can breathe in it because of the heavy use of disinfectant. As I write this on the steps of the Auberge, the sun is setting, there's a field and vine-covered wall complete with flowers – very pleasant.

July 31: Blois – Cheverny Vierzon – Bourges.

As we left Blois, a heavy mist shrouded the whole city, and the buildings and spires were blue and hazy. We stopped at the bridge for our favourite *chocolat et croissants*, then went on to Cheverny with its 16th Century Château where people still live. The rooms are about as fancy and French as possible.

At Vierzon, we suddenly got the bright idea that we'd like to be on the Mediterranean, immediately! We cycled on to Bourges and got tickets for Nîmes on a train, which left at mid-day. We were exhausted and it was so crowded that we had to squat in a doorway where – to make a long story short – we slept though our change of trains and had to spend that night on the floor of a little country station with four French girls who'd made the same mistake. We weren't good company, and quickly went to sleep on our sleeping bags.

August 1: Nîmes

Next morning and back on the right track (as it were), we went through green mountains, the most beautiful countryside I ever expect to see – villages with little mission churches with their bells, grey and white stucco houses with orange-tiled roofs, ruins perched on the tops of mountains and tiny rivers winding away in the valleys.

Nîmes itself is the most gorgeous little Roman city, built by the Romans to last. They still use the coliseum, and tomorrow I see my first bullfight here. The sunlight is extremely bright, the colours are brilliant, the sky a new colour of blue, and the girls are an attractive lot, to say the least. We're staying on at the Auberge, and will investigate this truly unique and beautiful city in some detail.

August 2: Nîmes

One of the best days I've ever had in my life! We biked into town for our *chocolat et croissants*, then set off to the Pont du Gard, the Roman-built aqueduct about 20k from here. We were awestruck at this edifice, which originally ran slightly downhill to Nîmes for over 30k. After exploring the aqueduct, we went swimming in the crystal clear river under it. The sun was blazing hot, and I can't remember ever having enjoyed a swim so much.

Back in Nîmes, the big afternoon – Bullfight Day! – and we had tickets. Can't explain the thrill of sitting in the 2,000 yr. old arena watching the deadliest, most dangerous and romantic of all sports; and with the help of another bottle of wine got carried away with the crowd in the bloody thrill of seeing eight bulls meet their masterful conclusion. Only two kills were a little nasty, while the other six were the cleanest, most dignified and perfect things I have ever seen. I loved the whole thing. Afterwards to the café, then back to the Auberge.

August 3: Arles – Marseille

Very good cycling to Arles, Van Gogh's hangout and another Roman city with an even larger arena, theatre, cloister, museum, etc. After lunch, back on the road and finally! – my first look at the Mediterranean. How gorgeous it was, and how exciting to see the sea again.

We took a shortcut over a mountain pass into Marseille, but unfortunately the Auberge was on the other side of town, about 30k, it was already getting dark, cobblestones all the way, insides are permanently shaken and will never be the same. Lost our bread and cheese en route and went to bed with no supper.

August 4: La Ciotat – Petits Four

Next morning we biked to La Ciotat, a gorgeous summer resort where we got terrific tans and now look like the rest of the sun-baked bodies along the coast. About 4 p.m. we biked on to Petits Fours, whose atmosphere consists of tables under the trees, friendly groups, a guitar playing – except for the usual bad toilet facilities, it couldn't be more pleasant!

August 5: Petits Fours – Toulon, Hyères – Le Lavandou

After pitched battle with ants in our tent at Petits Fours, we biked into Toulon, surely one of the most beautiful seaports in the world, with vast modern apartments, old buildings for character and a harbour filled with yachts. On to the beach at Hyères for another luxurious picnic and swim; and then on to Le Lavandou, where everyone was young and beautiful and naked. It had no Auberge, so we ate supper on the beach and slept there all night.

August 6: Le Lavandou – St. Tropez

We woke to find ourselves in a little sandy cove in the heart of a mountain-ringed ville, from which we cycled to Cavliar with its thousands of villas and hotels cascading down the mountainside into a cove filled with yachts, a splendid beach, and the finest clear blue warm water I ever expect to swim in (I've been in about 12 times!).

On to glorious St. Tropez, physically radiant in the almost unbearably hot sun, where we sat on the docks drinking beer and watching the passing parade. The big attraction is the yachts – sleek and rich, one even had a car fastened on top of it. We shopped along the narrow streets – how I wished I could buy something for everyone, but there's no room on my bicycle.

From St. Tropez, inland for 16k, straight uphill (which put me in a very bad mood) to La Garde Fresnet, a medieval town built in 1397 as a lookout for Saracen invaders. The water is non-drinkable except for one fountain in the centre of town where everyone goes with their jugs. It is, I might add, the best water I've tasted in France, with about 2 dozen trout in the fountain to keep it clean.

Walking through town, I noticed how old and dirty the houses were; but the streets were clean, and the insides of the houses seemed spic and span. This evening, the villagers were preparing for the festival next week. Our Auberge has no W.C., the bushes have to do, but loads of attractive women are wandering around me as I write.

August 7: St. Maxim – St. Raphaël – Fréjus

This morning, after delicious chocolate, we coasted back down the hill into St. Maxim for provisions and beer in the square, then on to St. Raphaël for more sun and cold beer, until it was time to push on to the Auberge at Fréjus. What a surprise! – the best one yet, with showers, decent beds, good cheap meals, and running water. We ate well and drank beer as the sun set behind a magnificent mountain.

August 8: Fréjus

Fréjus is so good, we decided to stay two nights. After breakfast, we went into town and saw another aqueduct, a Roman theatre where 'The Marriage of Figaro' is playing, and the 3rd of France's Roman coliseums. To my delight, an 8-bull corrida takes place tomorrow, so we will stay a 3rd night as well.

We biked on to St. Raphaël where we ate our picnic lunch on the rocks of a cove and watched some boys taking pornographic pictures of their girlfriends. What fun – a floor show for lunch! Then back to the *plage* at St. Raphaël for sun, salt water and *citronade* before returning to the Auberge and supper.

August 9: Fréjus

Today I'm 23! I don't feel any different. After a morning work detail of floor mopping, we biked into St.Raphaël, window shopped and visited the market, then to Fréjus for swimming, beer, and the Corrida. It was a fight I'll never forget; absolutely savage bulls and none of the toreadors escaped unscathed, although none were badly hurt. Very exciting, I'm really fond of bullfights.

August 10: Fréjus – Cannes

Today marked the last leg of our bicycle journey, a trip I recommend to anyone physically able to travel this way – I'll never forget the trip, ever.

We climbed down a cliff to a little cove where there were inlets and coral reefs to explore with Pigot's mask. One such reef was just like a natural carved swimming pool and was magnificent to see underwater with the mask. It had a sand floor and three sides of red coral. The other side opening onto the ocean. I had a great time swimming alongside the minnows and racing with them. But when I came face to face with what looked like a large skate, I came to the surface immediately. It was grand fun though. Then on to Cannes for an excellent lunch on the waterfront with its thousands of yachts, one of them Canadian! There was no Auberge, but a Tourist Office found us a place for two nights each, with 1 Breakfast & Dinner ($6. Can.), so here we are. We're both starved, but were too late for dinner tonight and 4 miles from town, so starved we'll stay.

August 11: Cannes

This morning at breakfast, (in my shorts and dirty shirt), a woman snickered at my appearance, and someone else remarked that "I can't imagine him being a Canadian lawyer!" Very rude, I must say. We spent the rest of the day at the beach in Cannes, sweltering and swimming. Then we went to see the yachts that we didn't see last night; and among them were Lord and Lady Dockers' calypso and also Trujillo's mammoth cruiser – the fellow from the Dominican Republic who gave Kim Novak the car. Afterwards we had a gorgeous feast at some restaurant and then to the beach where we sweltered and swam.

August 12: Cannes – Grenoble

Last night's dinner was okay and today we put the bikes on the bus and headed for Grenoble through the Maritime Alps and Low Alps, my first look at real mountains. Breathtaking roads with hairpin turns and sheer 1000 foot drops and little villages and rivers nestled below. Our route was the same road that Napoleon took when he returned from exile on Elba; quite a trip by horse, and it must have been agony for those who followed on foot.

At Grenoble, a pleasant surprise – my room is beautiful, with many shades of green and a huge picture window looking out through a mountain pass. The nicest place I've been in since I left Nova Scotia.

(From August 13 – Sept. 8, David was studying French at Grenoble and there are no entries during this time.)

September 8 – September 29: Italy

On September 8, I drove to Italy with a friend (Toto) and a friend of his called Giancarlo, and over the next three weeks toured the major northern cities, staying mostly in youth hostels (Ostellos), and seeing the sights with dozens of new friends made along the way:

Torino shocked me with its size and beauty, so modern

and so old. I'll never forget the Via Roma, lined with hundreds on hundreds of tall marble pillars."

Milano: I'm now as alone as I could possibly be, and rather enjoying the sensation. The Diary will be my company.

Next morning, however, "I had my pocket picked! 20,000 Lire, about 32 dollars. I'm so damned mad I'm going to leave Milan and head to Genoa!"

In Genoa, the Ostello was a reconverted castle on a cliff overlooking the Mediterranean, really gorgeous. We spent the afternoon swimming in the sea – my best swim ever. I'm starting to like Genoa very much – having the sea very near helps.

*   *   *

David toured Genoa and Nervi on the back of Angelo's Vespa (Angelo's Papa was president of Genoa's oldest bank, his uncle was head of the Harbour (whatever that means) and another uncle was a cardinal in Rome.

The next day, David and Corrine, a terrific Swedish girl, went to Rapallo, Santa Margarita, and Portofino, with its rickety pastel houses, little harbour filled with expensive yachts, and bazaars with prices for rich Americans.

Later that evening, David met Angelo's family: "What charming people, and so young; they pumped me full of cognac… and champagne, and Angelo made a speech – I was very touched. Back at the Ostello I was locked out, and had to climb over the wall."

"In Pisa we toured: the Baptisteria, the Duomo and the Leaning Tower, all splendid 12th century buildings, particularly the Leaning Tower. How strange to be walking downhill and going up at the same time!"

September 16 –18: Florence

Our Ostello is a fourteenth century castle once owned by Mussolini. It sleeps 400. Florence itself is crawling with treasures – the Duomo and Baptisteria (in green and white marble, unforgettable!), Michelangelo, Da Vinci, the Gates of Paradise and – most importantly – the Statue of David! one of the highlights of my life. So many treasures, so little time.

September 20, 21, 22: Rome

Started with High Mass at St. Peter's – the building of buildings, no question about it! Then Castel S. Angelo (aka Hadrian's Mausoleum), Palazzo di Giustizia, Spanish Steps, Trevi Fountain, Pincino Gates, Palazza Quirinale, Trevi Fountain, Pantheon, Victor Emmanuel Monument, Trajan Forum, the Palantine, ColiseumCatacombs, Vatican Museum, Trevi Fountain (yet again!!)...

September 23,24,25 : Venice

The Ostello, then St. Marks Square. First impressions of Venice: the best I've had of any place – a dream world.

September 26: Switzerland – Lugano

The Lugano Hostel is five km. out of town – the kind I like, rustic, musty, crazy bed, pretty main dining room, one South African fellow, three South African girls – straight out of *Macbeth* – two Irish nurses and two gorgeous German girls. We drank beer at a café where a man with no teeth played the flute and accordion.

September 27: Lugano

Today is the Lugano wine festival, with a parade, floats, bands, fireworks, boat races, etc. – quite jolly.

September 28, 29: Interlaken, no! Luzern, yes!

Started for Interlaken, changed my mind, went to Luzern instead. Had a midnight swim in the icy lake, then an excellent day with great weather. I have decided to leave tomorrow for London!

(David's Diary ends here.)

SOUTH AFRICA WITH PHILLIPA MONTSERRAT

A decade or more into law (1969), David's dear friend Phillipa Montserrat took him with her to the unimaginable lifestyles of her friends, the diamond billionaires of South Africa. David's diary of his three weeks in the laps and dining rooms of the very, very rich makes fascinating reading.

January 24: Halifax – Toronto

Left the office in the lousy rain took a half-empty plane to Montreal and Toronto. It still hasn't quite sunk in that I'm going to South Africa. Vodkas at noon, tea with the Laidlaws, Laurel's party (35-40 people), I didn't get tight, Madame did but not awfully.

January 25: Toronto – Airport

Spent most of the morning phoning friends (Cowans in Jamaica), Leon, Judith, Follows (Ted being domestic, Dawn the lazy slut in bed). Madame arrived at lunch, champagne, shopping for booze, presents, flowers and visit to Charlene, a girl with Hodgkin's disease, home to pack, taxi to airport, getting the Sara Lees from Laurel, phone mom, leave for England very drunk.

January 26: Trans–Atlantic Flight – London

Flight very smooth and pleasant with dinner, drinks, wine; Phillipa and I have hysterics trying to sleep foot to mouth. In London everyone is so good to us, we don't believe our good fortune. Check into Skyline Hotel at BOAC's expense; drinks (natch) and change our clothes; Madame must sleep; I phone brother Brownie (10 a.m. back home and he's not yet in!); sleep, shower and we're off to L'Etoile to meet Charles and Sonja Frend (he the director of *The Cruel Sea* and *Scott of the Antarctic*, have most superb dinner ever and delicious clarets, drinks, apple brandy.

January 27: Flight to Rome

As we're crossing the Alps, we hit turbulence, so violent I thought we were going to crash! Abject terror, trays of dinner and bottles of wine flying about! But after a few minutes things settled down, and the stewards/esses rushed to and fro putting everything together again.

Landed at Rome, and I found the Romans as surly as ever – never did like them! Back on the plane, another drink, then a sleeping pill (if we went down, I didn't want to know about it). Just before I went out, the pilot announced half an hour out of Rome that we had to turn back, a door some where hadn't closed, but with the drinks and pill and all, I didn't give a shit; when I woke up we were somewhere over Africa.

Dawn broke, magnificent in purples, magentas and citrus colours; and we were over Kenya, all lion-coloured, with little patches of abandoned farms which made me think of the Maus and the feckless settlers and their fates.

At Johannesburg we were four hours late; the confusion nearly had me undone, at least a dozen officials 'helping' us, and all one could hear was the loudspeaker asking Passenger Montserrat to go to one desk or another. The Sara Lee Brownies were lost, then recovered, and somehow we were swept into the last two seats on the plane for Capetown. Finally at eight o'clock, there was dear Patricia who swept us up and away through the sunset to gorgeous Vergelengen, the 8,000 acre estate and local showcase – even in the dark it had me gulping.

We went to Willa's exquisite little house, hydrangeas everywhere, priceless furnishings, superb dinner and service. I'm in my own guest cottage, attached to the main house. How can I describe it? It has two bedrooms, oil paintings, and beautiful appointments. Had a hot bath in the largest bathtub I've ever seen. Climbed the largest and most beautiful tree in the world. There are fourteen gardeners on this place, and with the sounds of Africa around me, I think I shall burst apart. I'm so excited and happy, what did I ever do to deserve this. I'm glad I'm tight at this point, or I'd just die. Don't unpack, just have a pill, and go to sleep.

January 28:

I wake up, throw open a window, nearly die at the beauty around me. Every window offers a new vista of unparalleled beauty. Where do I start?

Jock appears with a silver tray with tea and announces he'll return after breakfast to do my unpacking. He's very sweet, with his front teeth missing; he must be the valet assigned to me.

The pool, like everything else, is heaven. After the swim, we breakfast, and I meet Tom Barlow who will inherit all of this. He takes me for a tour of the farm part – 200,000 tons of peaches, 12 white families, 250 blacks, 200 casual workers. I nearly die when Tom announces he's an evangelistic missionary, and want to keep talking, but must go to Willa's for yet another superb meal – tonight it was crayfish and great wines – and conversation that is bright, witty, and at times downright rowdy.

Madame is out of it by nine p.m. – must have been a weighty day with ghosts and Ingestroms and all. Back to my cottage, for a walk: the sound of Africa, the sky – the stars are all different, and so many more of them – strange blackness...I don't walk too far.

January 29:

Jock unpacked me so beautifully, washing and pressing everything so carefully, wish I could take him back to Canada.

I'm thinking a great deal about Barlow...it's so inconsistent with the man I see that he should be an evangelist missionary – it's got to be a desperate crutch. Tom worked six years in the bush with the natives; has had two tragedies in his life – parents divorced and his beautiful 18 year old sister was burned alive in a home fire; has a wife and a little baby; is intelligent and less articulate than I am.

Tom says South Africa's two big problems are water and the blacks. Four factions: The English; the Africanners (Dutch Reform); the Blacks; and the Mixtures. Doesn't know a solution to the problem, nor believes anyone does. Capetown sounds like Halifax, slow pace, non-aggressive, somewhat sleepy. Johannesburg sounds like Toronto or Montreal. I'm intrigued with the place – wonder how I'd like to live here.

Every day starts with tea and a swim; then shave and wash up; then breakfast. After breakfast we went shopping then drove up into the mountains – breathtaking sights, a park where the flowering gum trees took me by surprise – imagine trees looking like giant rose bushes, only the blossoms were the size of hydrangeas. Then to a picnic area, where we drank bloodies, ate Cornish pasties and sausage rolls. Back down the mountain to a little area called Gordon Bay, where we swam at the most beautiful beach, bought wine and rock lobsters, and drinks in a sleazy bar. The waiter expressed interest in coming to Canada with me. I asked about his family. He said it was small – 5 kids. I can't manage that.

Phillipa and I dined with Willa – a superb dinner of veal cutlets, creamed asparagus and tiny new potatoes, passion fruit for dessert, then brandy and coffee and marvelous conversation, then Willa and P. drove me home. I'm sunburned, my poor nose frizzled and peeling, my hair is shades blonder, and I must say, I look quite well, feel great, and am deliriously happy.

January 30:

After breakfast I chatted with Tom's wife Ilsa, then we drove through the mountains to the farm of Louise & Peter Edmunsun, another beautiful estate (but nothing like Vergelengen, of course). Beautiful house, gorgeous lunch, good conversation, and my 'stories' went down well.

Later, we went to MorningStar to see Leonard and Dinky who was once pursued by the Prince of Wales (before Mrs. Simpson), and I loved her. He was the stuffy pompous English variety.

Back to Vergelengen for drinks, dinner, coffee and bridge. I had good cards but couldn't get together with either partner. Won both rubbers, but lost in points.

January 31:

Disaster – it rained this a.m. (bad for the peaches). We went to Capetown shopping, causing great anxiety for our hostess – doing something for ourselves, on our own! Phillipa thinks Arthur (our driver) has B.O., but he was hired for the day, so…We go to the shoe shop, the wine shop, the O.K. Bazaar land all those African bits of shit; then drinks at the Netherlands Club with Rolf (who advises me that as a lawyer I would earn approximately $7,000 a month); then home. Arthur nearly dies at the size of my tip ($3 Canadian).

February 1:

Into Capetown and do the cable car bit, which whips you up 3600 feet to the top of Table Mountain… what a sight! I marveled on the feeling of silence and aloneness that permeated the air – not hard to imagine you were at the bottom of the world.

The trip down was as terrifying as the trip up. Then we drove past Phillipa's old apartment, then Rolf's, then along the coast to the St. James, a sprawling hotel with true 1910 splendor, English upper class to the inch. After a gorgeous lunch, drove to Rolf's house in Hart Bay which was an individualist's hideaway, spectacular view and great gardens.

Ended at Maxim's, the Zebra Bar, saucy floorshow with a stripper (yours truly helped strip her, very funny), danced with everyone, then home and literally fell into bed.

February 2:

Phillipa and I spend the day sunning ourselves and cooking, as we've invited eight for dinner (those stupid maids nearly sabotaged my cheesecake by turning on the broiler every time my back was turned). Guests: Tom and Ilsa, Cynthia, Betty Janseen, Patricia, Phillipa, Willa and myself. It went off rather well.

February 3:

Having left a note for Jock to forget the tea, I sleep until nine o'clock. Breakfast with Cynthia and Betty the Broadcaster. Go to Willa's and pick up Phillipa, pack up for a picnic at the dam – about 14 people – the Morningstar crowd, Mrs. American Express and others I don't know. Smashing success – what organization. It lasts until dark. Back to the big house, everyone to bed, I to the pool where I lie on the diving board looking at the stars, then quietly into the pool, floating on my back, looking up at the southern cross. It's all too beautiful! What complete tranquility!

February 4:

Off to Gordon's Bay again for a swim. Never have I known such ideal swimming conditions. The Indian Ocean was perhaps 2 degrees colder than the air, which was dry, blazing hot, supplemented by a hot wind. Truly gorgeous. Dinner tonight was again superb, little game hens shot by Patricia, and chocolate mousse. Late that night I try to pack the car with Patricia, which ended up in tight lips and squint eyes.

February 5:

4:45 a.m. I am up and dress and finish packing with Patricia. We coffee and say good bye to Vergelegen. I am sad. Very sad. It's all been so happy. Pick Phillipa up at Willa's and say goodbye – very hard. She's been so kind. Thus the journey starts through the Cape, the wine district; the Karroo– an endless desert and finally the Big Hole and Oppenheimer's Stud Farm.

Tom and I finally got into 'life,' and Phillipa and I advised him that we have quite a different end of the stick from him. Both Tom and his mother suggest that I stay here. After everyone leaves, Phillipa does a neurotic bit I've never seen in her before – absolutely terrible, poor darling. Something that seems to be involved with this way of life and whatever is ahead of us in Johannesburg haunts her. I go home to bed, very upset.

February 6:

The Stud Farm is beautiful, a large pink palazzo, stroll round the garden part, then hit the road. Through the Busveldt, then the Transvaal, corn, corn, corn... feel sullen through all this, don't know why.

We hit Johannesburg and go straight to a 3,000 acre estate on the outskirts, owned by people called James and Betty Gemmill. The Madame is an old friend of Phillipa's, and the house quite beautiful, with tennis courts, a new swimming pool, and their own game preserve. Also two daughters – Anna and Judy – plus Geigla, girlfriend for the 6'8" son Richard.

After drinks, we meet the Master, a 6'4" gent in charge of hiring personnel for all the gold mines. He tells me quite candidly about the Negro situation, the four political parties, how apartheid isn't working, and that education of the blacks is the only solution, and integration must come. Then we dress for dinner at the Oppenheimers.

The Oppenheimer garden is a fairyland – terraced grounds, lit unbelievably, gardens without parallel. The house leaves me speechless; never in my life do I expect to see more beauty in terms of piss-elegant rich formal – beyond belief. The Goyas, Picassos, Dufys and Annigonni's portrait of Bridget Oppenheimer – literally dozens of priceless treasures.

The party is given for James, and includes an American couple called Meen, Punch Barlow (Tom's father and Cynthia's ex) and his new wife, a greasy-haired boy, a Christie's man and his wife, some others, and us.

The dining room is as breathtaking as the living room. The candelabras are as good as the cutlery. Dinner is served on the Romanoff service – gorgeous, the crystal heavy, the service beautiful, dinner delicious, conversation not bad, and Bridget Oppenheimer's diamonds something else – the one on her finger was gigantic, I couldn't stop staring. After dinner the women go off to another room and the men smoke cigars and discuss this and that. Then we join the ladies and another drink on the terrace. I walk around the grounds in a hazy dream, chat with Ms. Oppenheimer and the Yanks, then home. Phillipa is at Hy Nanny; I'm with the Epsteins, a charming doctor and his dear wife, in their spare room.

February 7:

After breakfast with Patricia in her charming little house, Betty and Phillipa arrive with the chauffeur, and we shop, then return to Hy Nanny. I have a lovely room, and share a bath with the three girls. Drinks, lunch, swim, walks round the garden, more drinks, then we dine. James and Betty Gemmill are most engaging and charming, informed and intelligent; and after dinner, it turns into a little party in the sun-room. After a walk and a chat by the pool, I turn in at 11:30 (just as the sisters return from a party in Pretoria).

February 8:

Phillipa, I and others go to the Lion Park and see ostriches, buck, wildebeest (gnus), lions, hawks, sables, etc., then back home to change for lunch and afternoon shopping. This evening we have drinks and dinner at Patricia's – a splendid evening with much laughter and frivolity.

February 9:

We shop in the morning and visit the famous Joan Lindberg. Baroness Von something and Barbie someone both appear and we have bullshots in the Gazebo and I get quite tight. After lunch we decide to go to Lindberg's girlfriend's country place in the bushveldt for the night... only a flash flood makes the road like Vaseline and forces us home. We sit under a magenta sky for a drink and go to bed early.

February 10:

Up to Brentthurst (the Oppenheimer's place) and spend the morning there, photographing, swimming and sunning.

I'm at their pool, the most beautiful I have ever seen and not a soul is there. Then taken to Bea and Solli Ornstein's for a smashing lunch. Phillipa gets to see Tim, an original Uncle Tom. Then on to Peter Fraser's for drinks and swimming, and home again to change for the family party at Fraser's, which goes very well. I dance a lot.

February 11:

Spend the day at Hy Nanny in much needed rest, swimming and sunning; then into my dinner jacket and to the Waddels' (Oppenheimer daughter) for drinks, joined by Bridget. The Waddels' home is ultra contemporary and I'm most impressed with them. On to the Iron Home – they're all there. It's James and Phyl Rudd's party and all the gowns and jewelry, ghastly dinner, bland entertainment, drinking excessive. Best part of the evening: Patricia. I shall never forget her trying to get those rhinestone pants off the bewildered lady in the white dress. Two older ladies, either of who could keep me in style for life so I am told, proposition me. At 1:00 a.m. a very tight Patricia takes me back to Hy Nanny.

February 12:

Departure day. Anna wants to come with me. Somehow I get packed, say goodbye, get out to the airport. Patricia's last words: "get those two the hell out of this country!" We're mysteriously 50 kg. overweight. The flight to London is mostly under sedatives, the best way to travel. Phillipa's remark about "the food trays prepared and packed by emerging African states and covered by pubic hairs are a far cry from Maxim's," and keep me laughing for 20 minutes.

February 13:

We check in at the Cavendish and after an exciting day shopping, we are now undoubtedly 100kg. overweight. Drinks with Charles and Sonja Frend and Donya Peroff, then a great dinner at L'Etoile, back to my room with Donya for more booze, then finally to sleep.

(The African Diary ends here.)

THE BASTION BEAVER

_____

During the 1977-78 season at the Bastion Theatre, in Victoria B.C., Artistic Director Ed Stephenson found himself floundering over what unwritten 'piece of stage business' he could possibly give to David Brown and Ron Halder during a particularily quiet section in the play, 'Automatic Pilot.' David Brown's immediate suggestion was "I could give him an enema!" Hence was born The Enema News, *later to become* The Bastion Beaver, *a company gossip sheet published and edited by David and Alison MacLeod.*

Issue # 1

BULLETIN:

Ed Stephenson's Cocktail Party Boffo
Show Biz Coup of Victoria Theatrical Scene!

On Monday night 'Fast Eddy' Stephenson, as he's come to be known off island, threw the surprise bash of the season at his penthouse apartment on Quebec Street, where at least eighty celebrities drank, ate, danced, sang and gossiped their way into the small hours of the morning. Seldom seen on this little island, 'Fast Eddie' surprised his guests by standing next to a bottle of gin for a good two hours without taking a drink.

The small, tastefully furnished apartment had been completely redecorated for the occasion. We loved the plaid sheets on the bed. Eddy, too bad about the stick up, that unfortunately drove people screaming from the bedroom and onto the already crowded balcony. Several people unfortunately used the occasion to make out with a number of the guests (you know who you are and so do we) but these isolated incidents couldn't possibly mar what was otherwise a sparkling evening.

Confirm or Deny

What noted Canadian Designer (M.E.) was seen on Sunday night (Sept. 16th) to execute a classic LURCH whilst attempting an exit from the elevator at the Queen Victoria Inn. Too bad it was only seven o'clock in the evening. A classic case of someone over discovering...but so early in the day!

Noted Canadian baritone, actor, bon vivant and tap dancer (J.N.) was purported to have slipped across the border for a dirty week-end in Seattle. Imagine his surprise when customs and immigration wouldn't permit him to bring his *animeaux d'amour* back to Canada. Tough luck J., but we've got enough of those cute little critters in our own back yard. Watch the toilet seats gang!

Curly headed vivacious mime artist (S.N.) surprised the

hell out of everybody by complaining about the high heels he has to wear for his fandango in Bastion's next production. One would think he'd be used to high heels by now, since he's well known in many local after-hours *boites* for his appearances as Marie of Rumania. Back on the stilts, S. We love you in spite of everything!

Former convicted drug addict (R.U.) had better watch himself. Bleeding to death from the eyes is no fun! But no question about the gold star on his chart for 'staying power'! He has surprised the hell out of west coasters by actually staying with one woman longer than his usual twenty minutes. Well done, R.U. ! You're number one with us in the race for the A.D. of the St. L.C., even if you are number 37 in everyone else's.

Talk about staying power! R.U.'s assistant (you're a caution, M.) has managed to stay in his chair for eight hours a day for a whole week. The question on everyone's lips is: when does he finally snap and run screaming from the rehearsal hall yelling, "I hate the lot of you, you miserable sons of bitches". It's O.K., M. You can let go. We'll understand.

Is there any truth in the contention that actress J.L. plugs into a live socket prior to leaving her house each day? Is her hairdresser really the same one who does Elsa Lancaster?

Ingenue L.C. had better watch out where she's putting her hands on A. Director, E.S. She might wake the sleeping tiger. Warned about this, she was heard to exclaim, "Balls, I'll put my hands where I bloody well please." TSK. TSK L.C.!

What frog prince has been hanging out at room 512 at

the Q.V. Inn, and why is he there? When it was suggested to him... "But she's twice your size!", he replied, "hit duzzin madder. He'll make two trips!"

What noted Welsh artist (W.S.) has recently developed an ear infection. Could it be from pressing it against a dirty glass held up against the partition wall between her suite and suite number 510! And what is going on in suite 510? Does dashing triple threat R.W. really have a mystery guest chained to his bed? This would account for the ear infection and the smirk on R.W.'s face. Which we're all getting sick to death of!

Former monk and religious mystic # (C.M) has been somewhat pushy in letting it be known that he left the monastery years ago and is no longer celibate. Won't someone please knock on his door. And where is the ladies' committee when you need them?

What's with R.M.? No one can be that talented, good, genial, generous, warm, funny, lovable, kissable and cute! Bullshit. What are you really up to when you leave rehearsals? Is your preoccupation with removing the wings from insects indicative of something we don't know about! Come out of the closet R.M. We don't care, we just want to know.

Why do noted linguists G.R. and P.R. converse in a foreign tongue when anyone is around them? Something to hide maybe? Watch out G.R. and P.R., your 'tongues' could get you in a lot of trouble. And why has P.R. suddenly developed a taste for lederhosen? And why is G.R. always smiling?

No wonder V.B. was chosen to play a role, which demands that he spend so much time in bed. Confirm or deny that V.

spent six months in Amsterdam studying the variations manageable in the horizontal position. What might he do if he ever gets vertical?

As for C.B. and P.M.! What curled her hair, and why is he hiding behind that? You can never fool the editor of this paper. Watch yourselves because we're watching you! Just because Christmas is coming doesn't mean that you have to get into the act!

As for the Saint, D.E.B, there was absolutely no information about him at the time we went to press.

Meals on the Road

Many people have written in looking for cooking tips for those who are endeavoring to survive on two burners, a frying pan and one pot. Here are some helpful hints, from a few survivors:

1. Eat out as often as possible.

2. Take full advantage of the women's committee dinners, bun fights and wine and cheese parties. At the latter functions, never leave until all the cheese is gone. Cheese is a great source of protein and costs the earth. A good belly-full of women's committee cheese could keep you going for days.

3. Cultivate the friendships of all locals. Try and look as hungry as possible as you ladle on compliments about anything you can think of. If this doesn't get you an invitation to dinner, don't be shy, ask them for something to eat.

4. Hey! It's that time of year. Take advantage of the many

fruit trees, burgeoning with fresh fruit in the Victoria area. Don't be shy about trespassing on anyone's property. We maintain that if it's good enough for worms, it's good enough for actors.

5.   There's fresh food on your balcony! Open your drapes slowly when you get up in the morning and you will see Sam Seagull perched on your rickety railing. Slowly place chunks of doughy bread in front of him, leaving a trail from the balcony to your open oven door. When the greedy, unsuspecting seagull finally enters the oven for that irresistible last piece, quickly slam the oven door shut and bake at 300 degrees for a good three hours. We call this recipe Seagull Hansel and Gretel. You'll love it. The seagull is a versatile creature. Great in sandwiches. Seagull fricassee is unbeatable. Cold seagull salad is a winner at any dinner. And shake and bake seagull will surprise, delight and totally fool your guests. The seagull is a large bird and for the budget minded, simply can't be beat at the price.

My personal favorite recipe for this feathered delicacy I've called Seagull Lucullus, after the Roman Emperor who just couldn't get his fill of Gull. Having captured your gull, keep him in the oven for three days with no food or water. Then give him a dish of Epsom Salts. Leave unattended for another day. The Gull, having been thoroughly cleaned out, will be grateful for the onion, carrots, and bay leaf you then provide. You then turn on the oven for three hours at 300, and presto. Baked Gull, aromatized from the inside. Delicious. Good luck. Keep those letters coming in.

Watch Next Week For:
– Wenna Shaw tells all
– Robin Ward's recurring nightmare

– Exclusive interview with a well-known transvestite
– Ed Stephenson: "I thought I'd go mad from the itch"
– Why Michael Egan over-discoed

STORIES & MEMOIRS

RONNIE BURKE

One of the first friends I ever had was Ronnie Burke. We lived in the same building; our family in the ground floor flat, his in one of the two upstairs flats. He had a brother called 'Azzie', nicknamed so because he had asthma and he never got out of his bed, which was in their kitchen; I suppose it wasn't so lonely for him there. Every now and again I was permitted to stick my head in their kitchen door to look at Azzie. He was a subject of great interest to a curious child, because I'd never seen anyone who never got out of bed before.

Ronnie had many brothers and sisters but as he was the runt of the litter, and much younger than the others, the older ones were not living at home with their widowed mother, so it was just Ronnie, his sister Nancy, and poor Azzie. Ronnie's mother was a very holy woman and sang in the choir at St. Agnes Church where we all prayed. When Mrs. Burke used to sing, Ronnie & I and Nancy used to giggle, because knowing her for some peculiar reason made us feel self conscious, as happens at the age of five or six.

Ronnie was the smallest of our gang, but the undisputed leader. He was the toughest and was always ready with the folded fist to 'plow' this one or the other. Also, he smoked at the age of five and he did have all those mysterious adult brothers, one of who was a taxi driver, and who was going to argue with that! He was also the boldest and the most daring; he knew all sorts of stories about Al Capone, Baby Face Nelson, and the other Chicago gangsters, undoubtedly learned from Azzie, and also knew about guns and explosives and all sorts of wonderful things like that. In the large garage on the property, which had been stables in an earlier time, Ronnie found one of his brother's tins of gunpowder. In a remarkable demonstration to me and the rest of the gang, Ronnie set the tin in the middle of the garage floor, stationed us outside, lit a paper match, threw it into the powder and ran out to where we were standing. We were so young we didn't have any idea what gunpowder was but we knew something wonderful was going to happen. In fact, nothing happened, so Ronnie went back in to see why. He looked in the tin and saw the paper match had gone out, but still had a glowing ember on the end. Pursing his lips he blew on the embers and...bang! He must have been lifted four feet straight up in the air, hit the ground with a thud and didn't move.

The rest of us stared in disbelief for a moment, then ran like rabbits for our respective homes and safe refugees under our beds. Didn't we just know that if we were caught we would all 'get it'! Besides, we'd all been forbidden to play with Ronnie. Even at five, Ronnie had earned a terrifying reputation. In fact, one of my friends, Dougie, used to threaten his mother that if he didn't get what he wanted he would go and play with Ronnie Burke. This usually got him his way, and he'd play with Ronnie anyway.

But I mustn't leave poor Ronnie on the floor of the garage like that. The explosion drew loads of adults to the scene.

Ronnie was sent to the hospital and released about a week later. If he hadn't been a hero before, he sure was now. The explosion burned off most of his hair, including, of course, the eyebrows. What a sight! And such a skinny, knobby-kneed little fiery furnace he was.

His smoking habits were of great concern to Sister Agnes Bernadette. Constant notes and visits back and forth from the house to school between poor Mrs. Burke and the good Sister could do nothing. Most of his cigarettes were found in the streets in the form of butts. If he could find three or four large butts in a day, that was a good day; but the best days were when Azzie would give him one or two whole cigarettes. Needless to say, the asthmatic Azzie smoked like a stove. One day, at school, just after the bell rang and everyone was in their seats, the lessons had begun and all attention was on sister, in through the front door, and late as always crept Ronnie. It was the dead of winter and all he had on was a cotton shirt, open to his chest.

"Ronnie Burke, you're late again. What's your excuse?"

"Sorry, Sister," barked Ronnie.

"Come here", she said. "You've been smoking again. You smell like a furnace." With that she picked him up, turned him upside down and shook him until a butt fell out of his shirt pocket.

"C'mon Sister, that's my last butt" argued Ronnie. Sister was having nothing to do with that. She took him and the butt to the window, (he struggling to retrieve it,) opened the window and threw it into the snow. She then picked him up and dangled him out the window so the tobacco smell would blow off him.

Coincidentally, at that very moment, Mrs. D'Arcy, mother of fourteen and living in a two-room bungalow directly across the street from our classroom, was at her front door calling for their dog. "Here shit! Here shit!" she called. The dog was called that by the kids because of his peculiar colour, and would only answered to that name. By this time, the classroom was in an uproar, some screeching with laughter, others taking up Mrs. D'Arcy's cry, and some just hootin' and hollerin'. Sister had to let Ronnie go to his seat finally and close the window, and in a matter of seconds had everything under control again.

One of the traits that characterized our gang was the constant seeking out and construction of hideouts. The need to have a hideout sprang from Ronnie's knowledge of Chicago gangsters; apparently, they always had a hideout, although I doubt that theirs ever resembled ours. Having found and established our hideout, it was necessary for each of us to pass the initiation, which was usually something diabolical hatched from the mind of our undisputed leader, Ronnie Burke. He always did it first, whatever it was; or else you had to be able to match him in some kind of endurance test. In this way, even at that young age, Burkie was establishing himself and constantly proving himself as the toughest of all.

I particularly remember my earliest and most colourful initiation, for which I was the first up. There was a long stretch of railroad track just before the train passed Simpson's Department store. The idea was (remember, we were about five years old at the time) that Burkie and I, in that order, would stand on the rail while the train bore down on us, and jump at the last minute. If the initiate (in this case me!) jumped before Burkie, that meant cowardice and you couldn't be in the club. And that would be worse than death, torture...anything imaginable.

The train bore down on us. And clever little pixie that I was even then, I knew that I didn't have a thing to worry about because the train would hit Burkie first. And then all I'd have to do was jump if I saw him get hit. (Not really so smart since we were standing side by side). But then the unexpected happened. The train braked! A moment of realization that there were adults on that train and they were stopping on our account. They'd be mad. (An exchange of panicked looks and then flight.) The other members of our gang were already hightailing it in all directions. I ran straight ahead at right angles to the train and eventually ended up in the men's washroom at Simpson, terrified beyond description. Burkie, less wise than brave, ran parallel to the train and was scooped up by the engineer riding the caboose. I remember him screaming, "Run Brownie, Run!" as he was being dragged away to what I was certain was incarceration and eventually death. While I was hiding out in Simpson's facilities I kept hearing what I thought were Burkie's last words, "Run Brownie, Run", ringing through my ears. I was so moved that his last thoughts should have been for me. Was he not a true leader indeed! It also crossed my mind that under the third degree, he might confess who the other person was. This unsettled me somewhat.

What in fact happened was that the police were summoned and Burkie was taken home to his mother who gave him a good hiding. But he never squealed on me, and thus has had my allegiance from that day to this.

One of the earliest hideouts I remember was located at the foot of our enormous backyard. It was constructed from packing cases that we had scrounged from somewhere or other, and it took us days to nail it together until we had it the way we wanted it. It was in fact a very complicated tunnel with a half dozen right angle turns ending up in a little chamber just large enough to contain eight little boys piled in and packed like sardines. Once in the tunnel, you couldn't turn round, but had to crawl right to the inner chamber, in inky blackness, and turn round in there. In the inner chamber were candles and matches, and that's where all our diabolical plots were hatched. The grandiose schemes we planned included bank heists, blowing up bridges and all sorts of grand things like that. We always settled for lesser escapes.

The initiation for this particular hideout was as follows. Burkie, the leader, would stay in the inner chamber. Each initiate would have to obtain two ten-cent boxes of wooden matches, crawl into the tunnel and sit with Burkie in the inner chamber. The two boxes of matches were then used as follows: you would open one end, light a match, shove it in the box and slide it shut quickly. This would cause all the matches to ignite and sulphurous fumes would squoosh out of either end of the box, filling the inner chamber, and render the people sitting there gasping, writhing creatures struggling for oxygen.

If you could sit there to the count of ten, (that's as high as any of us could count) you could be in the club. If not…too bad. But my friend Ronnie just stayed in there for one initiation after another. When the whole ordeal was completed, he crawled out into the sunlight, his face blackened with sooty tears, his eyes redder than glowing coals, and blind for about twenty minutes.

I remember him dramatically running around the backyard, fists in eyes, screaming, "I'm blind, I'm blind." We all thought it a wondrous thing, indeed. And what a leader! To sacrifice his eyes for the cause of the club, not to mention what he must've done to his lungs. His initial attempts to breathe on emerging from the 'hideout', sounded exactly like his brother Azzie in the middle of one of his worst seizures.

Nestled into our hideout, we hatched plot after plot, few of which became actuality, but I do remember one that did. Of all the many miraculous things that Burkie knew about, he had some knowledge of chemistry. Each club member was sworn to bring a lightbulb and an egg to the next meeting, which we all did, obeying Burkie blindly, to the letter, as always. With a file, he laboriously filed off the metal base of the bulb, leaving what he described as the basis for the bomb! We then broke our egg into our bomb and were required to pee into it.

The next time I was ever 'required' to pee was during a physical examination, which we all had to take at University. The stern nurse pointed to a shelf with a lot of odd-shaped bottles on it and ordered me to "fill one of those bottles with your urine!"

"From here?" I asked sincerely. After she left the room, I just couldn't do it. I've always been pee-shy. Fortunately another chap was in the washroom/office and I asked him if he'd give me half of his. Which he did... However, I digress.

Back to our bomb, the mixture of egg and pee. We then corked up in the bomb, sealed at the top in various ways, and then hidden in the hideout until the chemistry had happened. I don't know what the chemistry is, but I'll tell you that after a few weeks, 'putrid' barely begins to describe what these bombs were like.

When they were 'ready,' 'ripe,' 'explosive,' or whatever the term was, we waited for nightfall Friday. The drop-off place was to be from the Railroad Bridge, overlooking all the traffic, which was coming to and going from Simpson's Department store. I can remember being so excited about the night's mission, I nearly gagged on my supper.

Going out after supper was never something I could be absolutely sure of. It was always a carrot held out in front of me to encourage me to be a good boy. I was terrified that that night, which we'd been waiting for weeks, was going to be the night I wouldn't be allowed out for some reason or other. But fortune was kind, and off I went.

Most of the gang were already at the sewer with their bombs. I got mine; we waited for the last guys to arrive; then we crawled up the embankment, holding our precious secret weapons as tenderly and carefully as if they were newborn babes. Stealthily we crept along the tracks until we came to the bridge. The light from below shone up on our demoniacal little faces. One of the boys had a hat with a peak and earplugs and a drippy nose which he was constantly wiping with his mitten. These same faces of the night, phantom bombers, which that very afternoon had been at choir practice with the nuns!

On a signal from Burkie, we dropped our bombs one by one, and got about six cars. The explosions were very satisfactory, and I'm sure the mixture did little for paint jobs on the roof of the poor unsuspecting motorists. The cars were pulling over to the side of the road wondering what on earth had happened to them. Motorists were getting out and traffic was coming to a standstill. Finally someone looked up at the little figures on the bridge and began yelling threats and curses, which was our cue to make for the hideout. The traffic cop from the nearby intersection was on his way.

Later, crammed into our crawl space in the sewer tunnel, we recounted with glee every precious moment of the night's raid, and reveled in the success of our mission.

I can't remember when our little gang split up, or when it was that Ronnie Burke disappeared from the scene. Many years later I was returning from an evening at the library at Dalhousie University on the streetcar and there at the back of the bus, still small and wiry, was Ronnie Burke. I was thrilled to see him again; and learned that he'd gone to sea on a merchant vessel for a number of years and was now back in Halifax, working as a plumber's assistant, and was married.

That was a long time ago, and I've never seen him again. But I shall never forget you Ronnie… and hope you are well.

SISTER AGNES BERNADETTE
AND THE WAFFLE

S ir John S.D. Thompson School was divided into two halves, one for the Catholics and the other for the Protestants. I was in the Catholic half, and all I knew of Protestants in those early years of my education was that they took their recess period at different times from Catholics and we weren't going to be able to get into each other's Heaven when the time came.

Sister Agnes Bernadette was my first teacher, one of those many unsung heroines who devoted their lives to the cause of Christ and education. To this day I am grateful to those ladies for the solid grounding I received in reading, writing and 'rithmetic. They were fanatical disciplinarians, those girls, and with good cause – as Sir S.D. Thompson School housed a goodly number of roughnecks and toughs. From the four years I spent there, I can remember physical confrontations between the poor nuns and some of the larger lads. A couple of times blood was spilled. But the nuns always won. After all, they had God on their side – and that long leather strap with the metal strips on it.

One of the lessons that Sister drummed into to us daily was that of speaking what you had to say clearly and concisely without the aid of "umm," or "well," or "ahhh." Even "errrr" was not permitted.

All my life I've been nervous of transgressing this mortal sin of waffling whilst speaking, and am intolerant of anyone who does. If I do it myself, I'm sure that Sister's voice is going to come booming out of the heavens: "Stop waffling when you speak!" The result is that this early trauma has rendered me almost incapable of any sort of extemporaneous speaking at any occasion. If I don't have a memorized script, I simply can't do it. The fear of 'waffling whilst speaking' is too great in my soul. I learned the lesson too well.

Recently, I've thought about Sister again and again, because I've listened to so many people 'waffling' at various functions. One of my best friends does it in normal conversations to the extent that every three or four months I have to talk to him about it. His waffles take the form of "ehh", "agnns", "like-ahs", and "butt-ahs". When he's speaking he believes there must be no dead air from the time he starts until the time he's finished. I get the feeling that he never got to finish a sentence when he was a child, and now, once he's got the floor, he's not going to risk anyone butting into his train of thought, and the physical way of keeping them from doing this is to waffle. Well, Sister Agnes Bernadette isn't letting him get away with it. Every three months he gets the lecture from her through me!

At a recent Toronto gala, a truly memorable event with an exclusive guest list of the top three hundred (and through a comedy of errors, me) the plumpishly pink and blonde hostess had occasion to silence the crowd and make known her feelings. As winning as she was, she waffled through her mercifully short speech with phrases such as, "seriously though," "eaggh" and, "but reahhly, though," and, "I really mean that, seriously, aghhh". I could not help but think of Sister Agnes Bernadette.

Some of my least favourite waffles, if not already mentioned, are: "you know what I mean", "and well", "well, anyway", "Oh yeah," and "see…what I mean to say is…"

The list is huge, in fact, and I'm sure everyone except public speakers who've had it trained out of them more successfully than Sister Agnes Bernadette did with me will know which ones invade their spoken dissertations.

The last time I saw Sister was at my father's funeral. The funeral parlour was divided into two halves. On one side was my father's wake. He had been very well known and loved. There were masses of flower arrangements and hordes of people in attendance. On the other side of the funeral parlour was a casket containing the remains of a very old lady who had obviously outlived all her friends and relations. In contrast with my father's busy room, her side was stark and bare, adorned by one dramatic light.

I was standing at the front door, greeting people, when in swept Sister Agnes Bernadette, completely at home and in command of the situation. I was very happy to see her. In the twenty-five years since I had last seen her, she seemed not to have changed her appearance at all. Still the same ruddy cheeks, white teeth, sparkling and alert eyes, and I believe the same glasses.

We exchanged hushed greetings and condolences, and she surprised me by telling me all she knew of what I'd been up to for the last twenty-five years. She leaned into the room where my father's remains rested, leaned at a few other nuns then scurried across the hall to see the lone vigil light and the unadorned casket of the old lady. Then she darted back to me, and indicated with her thumb towards the old lady.

"Must be a Protestant."

"Why do you think that?" I asked, surprised.

"They don't go in for it like we do!"

With that, she whipped out her beads and got everyone going on the rosary.

My father, blessed with the best sense of humour of anyone I've ever known, must've had a huge laugh at all of this from wherever it is you laugh when you hand in the dinner-pail, as he was officially a member of the United Church all his life.

THE
TREACHEROUS DINGLE

In the early fifties, in Halifax, Nova Scotia, long before the days of women's lib or single parenthood, there was a young lady called Bella Doyle. She was from a very poor section in Halifax County with few if any amenities. Children growing up there had to really assert themselves if they were ever to find their place in the sun.

Bella was a cheerful, large-breasted girl who had two passions: one was boys; the other was swimming. She participated in all the aquatic events open to her and she was very popular with the other contestants. A keen competitor, she was more gifted in the endurance races than the short sprints.

There was a five mile race, sponsored by one of the local newspapers, which was an endurance test for the hale and hardy because the waters of the Atlantic, even in August, could be fifty degrees or so. The first year it was instigated, Bella won. Her smiling face was on the front page of the paper, and the whole town was delighted for her.

The course of the five mile swim was laid out as follows: the contestants would jump into the cold waters of Bedford Basin, swim through the narrows which opened into Halifax Harbour, swim around Point Pleasant Park into the waters of North-West Arm and past the Tower commemorating Confederation, which was always referred to by residents as The Dingle, then past the various boathouses and Clubs until the finish line at Public Baths. It was an arduous swim.

For years Bella entered the race, and for years she was the undisputed champ. Her young children, three in all, would run along the shore shouting encouragement to their Mom, Miss Doyle, and one year they were in the photograph on the front page with the beaming and victorious Bella. The race and Bella's victories became as normal a part of summer activities in Halifax as was the Natal Day Parade.

One year however, poor Bella had to give up her swim after only three and a half miles because of severe cramps. It was a tough break, and everyone was very sorry for her.

The New Yorker, a magazine of which I was very fond at the time, used to reprint articles from small out-of-the-way places with editorial comments. Several months after poor Bella's unsuccessful bid for yet another championship, the following appeared in *The New Yorker*.

"Reprinted from the *Halifax Star*.

Today, in her attempt to swim the five miles from the shores of Bedford Basin to the head of the Northwest arm, the Dingle pulled out Miss Bella Doyle with cramps.

Editor's comment: 'And that's where it really hurts.'"

MURPH

Many years ago in Halifax, I had a cleaning woman whose name was Mrs. Murphy, but she preferred to be called 'Murph!'

Murph was only five feet tall, had a very square physique, a quick gait, and a pug nose. She wore her glasses perilously perched on the nub of this nose, and never removed her hat, even when she was scrubbing floors. She had a number of hats, but they all looked more or less the same. Navy blue straw with plastic berries or flowers and some net stretched across the brim.

Murph was a loquacious woman. It was rare to be in a room with her and not have her barking at you. But, I loved her. She would not only clean the apartment but she'd darn socks and make bread. She was born in Newfoundland and has raised a family there. I don't know what brought her to Halifax. I'm sure she told me, but I, like other listeners, had probably tuned out, as I often did with Murph.

On a particular Friday I had mixed several jugs of martinis and left them in the refrigerator prior to leaving for my office.

I explained to Murph when she arrived for the day, that eighteen people were coming at six that evening for cocktails. And I told her to please leave glasses out on the bar, and the door unlocked when she left as I might possibly arrive home later than my guests.

It was one of those progressive parties where drinks were at one location, soup was at someone else's home and the party wandered from house to house until a five or six course dinner had been consumed. (When I look back at those parties, it puzzles me to understand their popularity.)

I was late getting back to my apartment that evening, and from the number of cars parked outside I could see that most guests were there. From the gales of laughter that greeted me as I walked up the stairs, I knew they had not only gotten in, but mercifully had helped themselves to a drink.

When I walked in, no one took much notice of me, as all eyes were focused on Murph! Obviously she'd been into the martinis all day and was now sitting cross-legged on the piano, hat askew, her mouldy fur coat draped across her shoulders, telling at full volume, a filthy story about a camel:

"...de army private backed de camel up to de Colonel and he has a go at her! He looks at de private, who was surprised at dis and sez, 'well I guess dat's 'ow it's done ain't it?'

Dc private looks at im an sez, 'No sir, we usually rides de camel into da whorehouse in Cairo!'"

She then slapped her thigh and poured herself yet another martini from the half-empty jug at her side as the guests howled with laughter.

*   *   *

Murph was the most independent woman imaginable. Though she had family, and was getting on in years, she never considered living anywhere except in her own space. This particular space was a room in a large, somewhat run-down rooming house in an old section of town. The floors were covered in cracked linoleum. Everything creaked. The smell of disinfectant was overpowering. The inhabitants seemed to be broken people, mostly on welfare. But Murph didn't see it that way. It was her paid-for space. That's where she lived. Period.

Like clockwork, she'd arrive every Tuesday and Friday at 7:30 a.m. She was never late and she never missed a day. When she hadn't been there the previous Friday, I decided on Tuesday evening to call 'round to her room to see if she was all right. In the dim rabbit warren of a building, it took some time to determine which room was hers.

Every person I asked didn't know who Mrs. Murphy was. I knocked on doors and described who I was looking for, until one large lady told me, "Oh, you're looking for Mrs. Wood. She lives on the top floor, first door to your left at the top of the stairs."

I could feel the large lady's eyes staring at me as I rounded the top of the stairs and knocked on the door of 'Mrs. Wood's' room. I knocked several times before a familiar voice weakly said, "Who's der?" I announced myself and carefully opened the door, half expecting it to drop off its hinges. In the shadows of the square room I saw a very old dog of indeterminate pedigree lying on an oval, braided rug. He looked up at me, mildly interested. Then, with what must've been a Herculean effort, he pulled himself up on his front legs, pressed up his rear, stood for a moment, as if catching his breath, then very slowly ambled over to me, his tail wagging very slowly. As he approached with his head lowered, a little voice from the bed said, "Dat's Henry."

"I had a difficult time finding you. They tell me your name is Mrs. Wood."

"Mrs. Wood is me name, but I calls meself Mrs. Murphy."

"Oh. I didn't know." Any further questions in that area seemed pointless to me

Murph had obviously had a stroke. One side of her face was immobile. She looked terribly frail. It was a shock to see her so still, as she had always been characterised by her boundless energy. She'd been there for days, alone, too weak even to seek help, though I doubt she would have even if she could have. Even in this miserable state she protested that I get any help for her, stating that she'd be all right in a couple of days. She was never all right again.

I visited her in hospital many times during the next few weeks, and she loved to have someone to talk to. Unlike our association when she cleaned for me, this time I listened carefully to her every word. I was aware that she was dying, and that I might be the only person to whom she could tell whatever it was she needed to tell.

I learned so much about Murph on my visits to that hospital ward. When she was a girl she did the cooking on a fishing trawler, on which her father was one of the fisherman. Her mother died when Murph was too young to remember much about her. "She was good to me, I remember dat much."

She'd had an older brother called Danny. "He wouldn't have nothin' to do with fishin' so he worked in de lumber camp. His boss sent him out to snake logs at de and of de day. He shouldn't have done dat. It was too dark. Dey found Danny next morning under da front runner of da sled. The horse never moved. He'd fallen forward between de horse an de sled. The horse jist stood dere all night. Danny hands were all bloody from tryin' to pull hisself out from under de runner, but it didn't do no good!"

I learned that Murph had been married to a soldier named Wood and had had three children, Annie, Lawrence and

Sheila. Wood had apparently been cashiered from the army for drunkenness and when he returned home, disgraced, the drinking got even worse, and eventually, incessant beating of Murph and the children ensued.

My girlfriend came with me one afternoon to visit Murph, and Murph exhorted us to "tie da knot", explaining that marriage was the best that ever happened to a person. I couldn't understand how she could have said that, having experienced the life she'd known; but said, "I was one of de lucky ones."

I guess that for Murph, love did not include any expectations of the loved ones; only love for them.

One of the last things Murph said to me was that she wanted me to have Henry. Henry was not the best present I've ever had nor was he something I even wanted, but for Murph to give him to me was nothing short of sacred trust.

The last time I went to see her, I was told she'd passed away peacefully in her sleep.

"Was she a relative?" the nurse asked.

"I didn't even know her," I said.

ANN MARGARET

It was October. Skies were leaden over Edmonton, and traffic was heavier than usual as Jackie Eddy drove home from her women's committee meeting at the Mayfair Golf Club. By the time she pulled into her driveway she wished she had gone before she left, as her bladder seemed about ready to burst. It was agony to run from the garage to the back door.

Rushing through it, she raced to the downstairs bathroom. Out of luck. "Sorry Mom, I'm in here," was the reply from her daughter Louise.

"I'll never make it upstairs," she thought as she struggled to do just that and attempted the stairs cross-legged. It seemed like forever, but she finally got to the bathroom on the second floor and threw open the door. As she entered, she was distracted by a movement in the bathtub. One look... a scream... and she fainted.

Ann Margaret, aged ten, heard her mother's scream and sat up in the bathtub, clad only in her knickers and covered in panchromatic blood. She watched silently. Her mother's pale green ultra suede suit was turning a deep shade of green and moments later her eyelids started to flutter.

"Hey Mom!" said Ann Margaret, "You peed your pants!"

As her mother realized that her youngest daughter had not been carved up by some homicidal maniac in the bathtub, her fright turned to indignant rage. Through her tears she said, "Where the hell did you get that stuff?"

Ann Margaret explained that it was the stuff Uncle David used when he played Dracula. He had sent her a bottle of it, as well as half a dozen cherry-flavoured blood capsules.

That very afternoon, Jackie received a call from Ann Margaret's teacher. Apparently, during class, Ann Margaret had bitten into one of the capsules and let the red substance ooze out of the corner of her mouth and just sat there. The teacher noticed eventually, had a major freak-out, and fled the classroom in search of the school nurse. Ann Margaret was a heroine to the rest of her class but in real trouble with the staff. The teacher was almost hysterical when she finally talked to Jackie who assured her that Ann Margaret would never do anything like that again and that all blood substances would be confiscated immediately.

*   *   *

Ann Margaret is only ten, but already she's starred in her school play and has met the Queen of England, neither of which events has bowled her over. She's the fourth and last of my sister's children, having been an unplanned baby and a total surprise to all concerned. She was a lengthy pregnancy and a difficult birth; even then she was reluctant to leave a situation that contented her.

I think she's very beautiful, with seductive, sleepy eyes and a slight overbite that is reminiscent of Gene Teirney.

There's very little that goes on in her home that she's not either directly involved in or has a lot to say about.

Ann Margaret loves horses but hates boys, and hates dogs but loves men. She can be quite self-righteous in the presence of her parents, but when she's alone with her Uncle David there's nothing she delights in more than a good dirty joke. Years ago, she would go into paroxysms of laughter at the very mention of 'ca-ca poo-poo.' When Uncle David taught her to sing 'Swingin' on the outhouse door...without your pants on,' she went berserk. She couldn't wait to get to her friend Laura, the one with the teeth like a picket fence, and share this new-found obscenity with her. But that was long before she was ten. These days, she's showing signs of a new sophistication.

Not too long ago, her mother was driving her home from school when Ann Margaret's older sister Louise proffered the information that Pierre had actually kissed Ann Margaret.

"Is that true?" asked her mother.

"Yes," said Ann Margaret, "I nearly threw up!"

She's a very independent little creature and has always been able to handle herself very well on any in-fighting situation. Roughhousing has been a favorite playtime activity, and she wouldn't be put down by either direct confrontation or by important personages visiting her home. For instance, a few years ago she was sitting on my lap, being annoying and demanding attention. No subtle hints or persuasions of mine would dislodge her from her comfortable situation.

Finally, I barked at her, "Your teeth are scummy. Go upstairs immediately and brush them."

"Yeah," said the child, "Well you've got yucky breath."

Another time, Tom Kneebone, the brilliant comic and good friend of my sister's, was visiting them during a concert tour with the lovely Dinah Christie. As a special treat, Louise and Ann Margaret had been allowed to stay up late that night and go to the concert. The next morning, both little girls were lingering over their breakfasts hoping to see the famous Mr. Kneebone before they were sent out to play. They managed to outlast their mother's exhortations to get on with it, and were still at the table when a sleepy Mr. Kneebone arrived at last.

"Oh, Mr. Kneebone," began Louise, the more feminine and sweet of the two, "I just loved your concert. You looked so handsome in your white suit. And my favourite number, Mr. Kneebone, was when you sang 'Why do the Wrong People Travel.'"

"Thanks!" said Mr. Kneebone.

Ann Margaret, her face cupped in her hands, elbows on the table, had not taken her eyes off him during all of this, and a few beats after Louise had ground to a halt with the superlatives simply said, "Yeah, well I hated it!"

Tom's reaction was reminiscent of W.C. Fields' reaction to children, while Ann Margaret's mother, a woman blessed with a great sense of humour, collapsed with laughter.

But now that she's ten, as I say, she's become more sophisticated in her journey through life. On one of his recent visits to Ann Margaret's home, Uncle David had thrown a surprise party to honour his sister's birthday. The food was late in coming; and Ann Margaret had had about enough of this fete when she cornered Uncle David in the kitchen.

"Listen, would you do a favour for a short person?"

"Sure thing," said Uncle.

"Would you get one of those glasses down off the top shelf and get me a glass of milk?"

"Sure."

"I'm so tired and hungry! And of course I'll never get to sleep now."

Thinking it was because of the lateness of the evening, Uncle David said, "Why not?"

"Because I just saw a program on television about Jack the Ripper," explained Ann Margaret.

Uncle David became sentimental at this poor little girl being frightened by a horror film and said, "Never you mind about that. If you're frightened and can't get to sleep, you can just come into my room and sleep with your Uncle David."

She took a long look at this creep and said, with a toss of her long hair, "I'd rather sleep with Jack the Ripper."

The Queen of England was arriving in Edmonton for the Commonwealth Games and the whole of Western Canada was putting its best foot forward to make the games and the Queen's visit memorable. Western hospitality, if you didn't already know, is second to none. It had been announced on television and radio and in the newspapers that the Queen would be dining on a particular night at Government House, which is only a block or two away from Ann Margaret's house.

On the appointed evening, Ann Margaret decided that she would pay the queen a visit. She left the house and walked to Government House where the onlookers were assembling, picked a few flowers from one of the flowerbeds, then sought out an R.C.M.P. constable. In her most seductive and tantalizing way, she cosied up to the largest of these gentlemen who looked down at her from his great height and said, "Are those for the Queen?"

"Yes," said Ann Margaret, in her best imitation of her demure sister.

"Well, wait here with me and I'll see if I can't arrange for you to give them to her."

Meanwhile, Ann Margaret's sisters arrived at Government House to see the arrival of the Queen and were somewhat surprised to see Ann Margaret and the giant RCMP constable cordoned off in a little area to the right of the steps. Moments later the motorcade arrived. The Queen, smiling and waving to the applauding crowd, stepped out of her car, followed by Prince Phillip. Words were exchanged, and the Queen walked over to this urchin in dungarees, t-shirt and laceless sneakers, clutching the handful of stolen dahlias, and asked her, " Are those for me?"

"Yes," replied Ann Margaret.

"What is your name?"

"Ann Margaret."

"Thank you very much." And the Queen went forward.

The Duke of Edinburgh then approached Ann Margaret and said, "How did it feel, talking to a real Queen, Ann Margaret?"

"Neat-O, Prince."

Ann Margaret watched the royal couple disappear up the steps of Government House, and since there didn't seem to be much else happening, returned home to investigate the contents of the cookie tin, mentioning none of this to her parents.

Moments later, her older sisters stormed into the house, protesting to their mother that, "If Ann Margaret felt she had to meet the Queen, at least you could have had her wear a dress!"

The next day, half the newspapers in Western Canada published photos of Ann Margaret presenting the pilfered dahlias to the Queen. In the eyes of the world she looked like a little saint!

AUNT ETHEL
GOES TO COURT

I hadn't been practicing law for very long when I got a call from Aunt Ethel, the nun. She's one of my mother's many sisters and was always a great favourite of mine. She wanted me to write a letter for her, since I was now a member of that august fraternity who wreak terror in the hearts of anyone to whom a lawyer's letter is sent.

It turned out that poor Aunt had been in an accident, lost some teeth and was having persistent headaches. I persuaded her to come to my office and tell me the whole story, wishing to do the best I could for my mother's sister.

Aunt Ethel had been a passenger in the rear seat of Doctor Merrit's car when a large transport truck sped through a red light and occasioned the doctor to smash into the side of said transport truck. Aunt was hurled from the rear seat, across the empty seat in front and through the windshield, landing sprawled over the hood of the good doctor's car.

"Must've given her a nasty shock," I thought. And she was an old lady then!

After reviewing all the facts, it turned out that the lawyer for the truck's company, a good catholic, was advising his clients that as Aunt was a member of the Sisters of Charity, it was unlikely that anything need be done about her complaints and calls. Little did he know that Aunt had a nephew, a boy barrister, who was eager to champion the cause of the poor, down-trodden and smashed-up nun.

Before I could issue a writ, it was necessary to convince Mother Superior that just because Aunt was a member of the Order was no reason for her to abandon her civil rights. She had suffered a civil wrong and should seek redress from the courts just like anyone else. The heartless corporation was not getting away with this. And as for that Catholic lawyer representing them, well, I can tell you he was an English Catholic, not Irish!

Mother Superior was most understanding, and agreed with me, having only one reservation, that there should be no publicity connected with the case. I assured her that I would only proceed if I was certain I could obtain the assurance of both the judge and the lawyer for the other side that Aunt Ethel and the religious order would not be exploited over this case in any way.

The next problem was how to describe Aunt Ethel on the writ. She hadn't used her maiden name in forty years, and her chosen name in religion was not technically her legal name. My then partner-in-law, of the Jewish persuasion, solved the problem by using both her names in her description on the writ as plaintiff. As he was so taken with the matter, he also offered to lend his assistance to Aunt, free of charge. Lines of battle were drawn up, dates were arranged, prayers were said at the motherhouse for both my Jewish partner and myself, and a judge was drawn...the only Catholic judge on the nine man bench. Here, let me hasten to add that his being Catholic would have absolutely no bearing on the case whatsoever. It's just ironic that it turned out that way. My partner really did believe by this time that God was on our side.

The case, in fact, was simple and straightforward. The facts were easily proved, and there was absolutely no question of liability. The truck driver's insurers had to pay for everything. I might say that I was especially proud of Aunt Ethel on the stand. Not only was her testimony clear and linear, she spoke loudly. She also had a diary that she was permitted to refer to and she had noted everything in it having to do with the accident.

The only question was, how much? The judge went away to deliberate and all sides retired to, await the decision which came down some weeks later.

For purposes of telling the story, it is important to know that Aunt Ethel did not live in the large motherhouse, but was part of a small community of nuns in a downtrodden end of town. There were six of them in all, one of them being a kind of junior Mother Superior for their little community. They earned their way mainly by sewing and by teaching music. They were not an affluent little band.

Weeks passed and word was received that the decision was down. It was in favour of the plaintiff, for several thousands of dollars, both for the recurring headaches which medical experts had testified would in all likelihood continue, and for the out-of-pocket expenses and costs of the case. Everyone was pleased. In all fairness to the English Catholic representing the insurance company, he seemed as pleased as anyone else.

The next question, after advising Aunt Ethel of her victory, was what to do with the money. She hadn't thought of it but was obviously giving it some heavy consideration now. I suggested putting it in a bank account in her name. That was no good. They were not allowed to have anything in their own name. How about sending it out to the Motherhouse?

A definite no-no! I was about to just leave the problem with her and hang up when a flash of some sort struck her, and she asked me, "Could I have it in cash?" Certainly! "In small bills?" asked the little voice. Of course. "Then Dister and I will be down tomorrow afternoon."

The following afternoon, after I had arranged a bag full of small bills from the Royal Bank, Aunt Ethel and the junior Mother Superior of their little community arrived at my office at the appointed hour. I was beside myself with excitement, and bursting with curiosity as to what plans she had for the booty. It was none of my business, of course, and I should never have asked, but I hoped she might volunteer the information.

The two of them sat opposite my desk while I counted out thousands of dollars in small bills. It took a while. When I finished, Aunt looked at the junior Mother Superior.

"I've never seen so much money in my life, have you?"

"Never so much in cash," replied the other Sister, who hastened to add that she had seen cheques for large amounts like this.

Aunt Ethel then took from her purse about a dozen envelopes, addressed and stamped, and began paying a few bills. "This is for Sister Marie Claire in the convent in Sydney," she said, peeling off two tens and a five, "She loaned me that for my medication while I was down there."

"Oh, yes," said the other Sister. Another ten and a five were dispatched to some dentist who fixed a tooth; several tens and a twenty to another dentist for something more complicated.

"Its like Xmas!" I thought.

After several hundred dollars were dispersed in this fashion and all the envelopes were sealed she looked down at the pile left. "Now it comes," I thought, "Now I'll find out what's going to happen to the bulk of her fortune."

"Would you like a large brown envelope for the rest?" Yes, she would.

As the money was being stuffed into the envelope, Aunt Ethel looked at the other Sister and said, "Do you suppose we could have a little treat for tonight?"

"What did you have in mind?" said the other one, cautiously.

"A half dozen bottles of 7 Up," said Aunt, hopefully.

"I think that would be all right, in view of your pain and suffering and all."

"And a brick of ice-cream?" said Aunt, pressing her luck.

"Why not!" said the other nun, throwing caution to the wind.

I watched them bustling along the street from my office window, clutching the large brown envelope with the thousands of small bills, heading off for the 7 Up and the ice-cream, heading off for what was undoubtedly going to be a big night in the little convent. I thought of the money many times after that and imagined it was still in the envelope, in the pantry between the cookie jar and the flour bin, and when sewing supplies or other necessities were needed, the money would probably see them through for a long time.

About two years after this, Aunt Ethel was in another accident. This time the car was driven by another Sister, and Aunt was in the front seat. They were going down a steep hill, the brakes gave way and the two of them went straight through a plate glass window at the bottom of the street and into the reception area of a finance company.

But as she explained to me some days later, "It wasn't anything like the first accident! No one was hurt, and the people in the finance company gave Sister and me a cup of tea."

JIMMY BROWN

Jimmy Brown was only four years old when he first broke his mother's heart. He was the littlest of her four children, and like the other three, had a head of thick hair. Some people would describe him at that time as wiry, or spare. To me he was scrawny!

Jimmy Brown had a thin, raspy voice, and though energetic, was different from his siblings in his contemplativeness. When he was in a room with adults he was not a performer; even at that age he was a listener. It was nothing unusual for Jimmy to be allowed to sit in a room with adults for hours, because he sat quietly and just listened, his little blue eyes darting from speaker to speaker and taking in every word that was being said. He was a lad of few words, and great independence.

All my nieces and nephews had a particular year when they first began to be a person. Stories of Lynn, or Bobby, or Karen would start circulating in their particular 'coming of personality' year.

"Did you hear what Bobby did?" Or, "Do you know what

Lynn said?" would be the gossip 'round the kitchen table, or the subject for discussion at tea.

With Jimmy, it was in his fourth year that he emerged, like a butterfly from his cocoon, as the independent one.

His grandfather, affectionately known as Gramps, had a camp on an island in Sheet Harbour. It was Gramps' Shangri-la. The fish were plentiful, and in deer season there were plenty of those around too. Gramps had several boats and canoes, a couple of dogs, and an island paradise in an area of the world where no one else could build. It was his domain. He also had a passion for children, and especially Jimmy Brown.

It was late spring in Jimmy's fourth year that Gramps invited him to go with him to the camp. Jimmy quickly agreed to the invitation. He went immediately to the basement, carried a large suitcase of his father's up to his room, emptied the contents of his chest of drawers into it, presented himself to Gramps who was still having his tea with Jimmy's mother in the kitchen, and said, "I'm ready."

"You're not going to get all the way down there and decide you want to come home I hope," said Gramps in his deep, throaty voice.

"No," said Jimmy Brown.

"Won't you miss me?" asked his mother.

"No," said Jimmy Brown.

By the time Gramps finished his tea, Jimmy Brown was already sitting in the front seat of his car, waiting to go away from home for the first time, his suitcase having been deposited in the back seat of the car. His mother came out to say goodbye to him.

"You're sure you're not going to miss me?" she implored. He shook his head.

Now I must hasten to add at this point that Jimmy Brown has always loved his mother who is easily the most lovable person in the world, but he just wasn't going to miss her, love notwithstanding.

Two weeks went by and Gramps' old car returned to Jimmy Brown's house. Out came Jimmy, the suitcase, and Gramps, in that order. Jimmy's mother heard the car, rushed to the door, having missed her dour little independent while he was gone, and gave him a big hug as he entered the vestibule.

"Did you miss me?" she asked.

"No," said Jimmy Brown.

This was the first time Jimmy Brown broke his mother's heart. Not that he doesn't love her, he just wasn't and isn't 'missing' anyone!

During the year he became four, Jimmy's taste for driving cars became manifest. His other Grandfather, who was called Grand Dad, as opposed to Gramps, had just acquired a new car, of which he was particularly fond. It was a very large Buick, youthfully white with red upholstery. Looking out the window of his summer house one summer afternoon, imagine Grand Dad's surprise to see his large white beauty slowly leave its launching pad, accelerate quickly, and disappear straight into the woods. By looking very carefully, Grand Dad could just see the top of a white head behind and below the steering wheel. It was the most excited I'd seen him since he'd cornered the porcupine in the willow tree.

Jimmy thought the whole trip into the woods was 'keen'. The tow-truck man who eventually got the white beauty out of the swampy underbrush was glad of the fee he was paid for doing so.

In the fall of Jimmy Brown's fourth year he was invited to spend a Saturday night with his Uncle Donald, who was living in his parents' home about a mile away from Jimmy Brown's home. Uncle Donald was about nineteen or twenty at the time and, like everyone else, was enamoured of the young

Jimmy.

Uncle Donald's parents were away for the weekend and he had planned an evening around the television set with lots of things to eat. Jimmy Brown accepted the invitation eagerly. This was the second time he'd ever been invited anywhere. And some people had been a little frosty with him since his madcap race into the woods in the white beauty! He packed his suitcase, which had now been appropriated as his own, and seemed to go everywhere with him, including the corner store. His heart-broken mother drove him over to Uncle Donald's place after supper.

One word about Uncle Donald... he, like all the other male members of my family, is characterized by the quality of generosity, and believes that 'more is best'. No sooner had he shown Jimmy where he was going to sleep than he asked him if he would like a coke! Jimmy was agreeable to any suggestion. They settled themselves in two comfortable chairs in front of the television and the evening began. First an orgy of potato chips, chocolates, western movies, situation comedies, peanuts, ginger ale, popcorn, baseball, horror films, and finally, pizza and milk, and finally 'God Save the Queen.'

When there was nothing left to watch or eat, Uncle Donald looked over at his guest, who by this time was sound asleep, spread-eagled over the armchair, stomach distended and out cold. He picked the little body up, got him upstairs, into his pajamas and under the covers, then he himself retired.

About two hours later, around 2 a.m., Jimmy Brown woke up, sat up, and threw up. Looking around in the dim light and feeling less than perfect, he remembered where he was, and didn't want to be there any longer. He got out of bed, found his slippers, which Uncle Donald had thoughtfully left by the side of his bed, put his clothes into his friend the suitcase, and crept down the stairs to go home.

He was an unusual sight to see on a busy thoroughfare at

two o'clock in the morning – a little runt in his pajamas and slippers, carrying a suitcase almost as large as himself. Inevitably a number of motorists stopped to offer him a lift. But Jimmy Brown had been told by his father never to get into a stranger's car and so he refused not only their offers, but indeed, refused to talk to them.

As he approached the rotary, which marked the halfway point in his journey, another car stopped. This car was different in that it had a large red light on top of it. One of the two men in it got out and asked him where he was going.

"Home," replied Jimmy, not breaking stride.

"We'll take you there," replied the policeman.

Under protest, and after a promise from the policeman that he could see how the red light worked, Jimmy Brown was deposited in the back seat of the cruise car. He didn't know his address, but showed the police how to get to his house.

Jimmy Brown's parents were awakened from their sleep a few minutes later when the doorbell rang. His grumbling father went to the window to see who the late-night caller might be. He was surprised to see the police car outside his house, red light revolving. There, peering out the back window, the unmistakable white head of Jimmy Brown. Curious as to what might have transpired since his son went to Uncle Donald's, he went to the front door.

"Are you Jimmy Brown's father?"

"Yes."

"We found him near the Armdale Rotary."

The back door of the police-car opened, Jimmy and the suitcase came up his walkway, into the house, and as he passed his father on his way to his own bed Jimmy Brown simply said, "I threw up."

His father thanked the police for bringing the boy home. The police were not amused. Then his father phoned Uncle

Donald, a sound sleeper. After some time a sleepy voice answered.

"Where's Jimmy?"

"In bed."

"Go and see."

"I tell you, he's in bed."

"Will you go and see?"

Moments later, the sound of thundering footsteps down the hall could be heard through the receiver.

"He's gone! He's gone!" exclaimed the panicked voice of Uncle Donald.

"The police just brought him home," replied the father, and they all went back to sleep.

*   *   *

Fourteen years later I had occasion to live with my brother and his wife for a few months, and was eager to get to better know Jimmy Brown, now eighteen years old. Jimmy had turned out to be the driving force of his 'gang', very popular with girls, and a cracker-jack basketball player. Not a physically handsome young man, but tall, pleasant looking, thoughtful, polite, generous and charming beyond belief. I was really pleased with the way he was turning out, but somewhat concerned that he was doing miserably in school, due more to a lack of interest than a lack of ability. I took this concern to his father, my older brother.

"What can I do?" asked his father. "I can't make him study."

I certainly didn't know what the answer meant. But I went out, bought books, and tried to urge upon him the desirability of getting an education for its own sake. When that wasn't making much of an impression, I tried to persuade him that getting an education would allow him to choose what he wanted to do later on in life, rather than have life make the choices for him.

Jimmy always listened politely to these lectures in such a way that I knew he was being polite and not taking in a word I was saying. I suppose he'd heard it all before anyway. But, determined to make inroads, I invited him to dinner one night, and we would go to a fancy restaurant. All of which transpired.

We had a very agreeable dinner. Then I started in on him, which, I'm afraid to say, was only more of the old exhortations and cautions.

Jimmy interrupted me. "Uncle David, I know you're worried about me, but you don't have to be, because I've got what hardly anyone else has."

Somewhat taken aback, I said, "What's that, Jimmy?"

He looked me straight in the eye, leaned forward and said, "Supreme confidence in myself!"

Since then, I've never said another word to him about life, deciding that it was much better to enjoy him and encourage him in his endeavours whatever they might be. Sometimes I also wonder if, at any time in my life, I've ever been able to make that statement myself. In this case, the erstwhile pupil did indeed teach a lesson to the erstwhile teacher.

SUMMER STOCK

The Kawartha Summer Theatre Festival

'A Thousand Clowns'

The sun was shining. It was July. I was on my way to the Kawartha Summer Theatre Festival in Lindsay, Ontario, a quiet, typical small town about two hours north-east of Toronto. However, unlike other typical Ontario towns, it boasts a splendid theatre, which had nearly become a parking lot! Fortunately, sufficient townspeople had the wisdom to save the building from that fate.

I was playing the protagonist in Herb Gardner's 'A Thousand Clowns.' As I trudged down the main street with my suitcases, I ran into the producer, Dennis Sweeting, a man with the most amazing wing-like eyebrows and a great head of salt-and-pepper hair. He was running towards me with a twelve-year-old boy in tow who turned out to be my co-star in the production. As he passed me he shouted, "I'm just taking young Carl to the Mayor to get his haircut. I'll see you later."

"Why shouldn't the Mayor be a barber?" I thought. "Probably knows more of what's going on in town than the lawyer!"

At the dress rehearsal of 'A Thousand Clowns,' Dennis asked me if I'd like an audience to check the laughs. I agreed it would be desirable and the director was eager for this as well. The magic hour arrived, the curtain rose, then I appeared in my shorts, t-shirt and baseball cap and delivered my first line. Imagine how surprised I was to hear it repeated from the audience, loudly, and in a foreign tongue, followed by a mildly explosive murmuring from the small invited group.

I continued with the second sentence. Again, it was repeated, loudly, in a foreign tongue, followed once more by a mildly explosive reaction from our guests.

Bravely, but rapidly losing confidence in myself, I delivered my third line...the gag line. There was a loud repetition from my unseen competition and an even bigger and longer reaction from the crowd.

"Am I losing my mind? Is this really happening?" I quickly mused.

I continued for a few more sentences when I suddenly noticed from the corner of my eye that a small, black baby in white sleepers had crawled up over the stairs from the auditorium and was on stage with me. He looked at me, drooled, stuffed his fingers in his mouth and grinned impishly. I picked him up, and resisting the urge to hurl him back into the audience, sat down in the armchair on stage right and began to tell him the story of *Goldilocks and the Three Bears*.

The stage manager very cleverly deduced from this behavior that I had given up on the play and lowered the curtain. Within seconds, the Producer was advancing on me from stage right, the Director from stage left. Everyone was talking and no one was making any sense.

I shouted at them all to shut up! "What's going on out

there, and who the hell is he?" I asked, referring to the little black fellow in my lap who was bouncing up and down on my testicles, enjoying the confusion enormously.

The Producer began, "I'm very sorry David, I thought it was a good idea at the time, but…well… there are thirty-six non-English speaking Tibetans out there, and their Llama is translating for them."

There was a stunned silence, except for my little visitor, now wearing my baseball cap and rending the air with squeals of delight. For the first time in my life I was totally at a loss for words. At this moment, a little woman in a strange costume crawled under the lowered curtain, rushed over to me and snatched the baby out of my lap, baseball cap and all, and disappeared under the curtain again.

Timidly, I ventured to ask, "Why are there thirty-six non-English speaking Tibetans here?"

It was explained to me as follows: These poor people had been trapped somewhere in the mountains of Tibet, the enemy surrounding them on all sides and advancing rapidly, Lester B. Pearson decided that rather than drop Red Cross Aid parcels on them, he'd get them the hell out of there and resettle them in Canada. Half were brought to Lindsay and the other half ended up out west somewhere. The half in Lindsay had only been there for a matter of days when dear Dennis, our Producer, in a gesture that was more heartfelt than wise, invited them to come see our dress rehearsal.

I was intrigued and delighted with this explanation and I suggested that we get on with the rehearsal and to please ask the Llama and his group if they couldn't try to keep the noise down.

We began again! At the end of the first Act, Dennis announced to the Tibetans that it was all over, thanked them for coming, and hoped they had had an enjoyable evening. They didn't understand anything at all except it was time to go back to their billets, where they spent hours playing with the light switches... they had only just discovered electricity!

For years it had been Dennis' practice to hire some of the local people in the town to supplement the otherwise professional casts of his plays. This did two things for him; first it cut down operating costs, because the locals came free; and secondly, it stimulated local interest in the theatre to have the local dentist, barber gas attendant etc., in the productions

Vince, the postman, played my older brother in 'A Thousand Clowns,' ...my really old, older brother, as Vince was about thirty-five years my senior. He had a huge speech at the end of the play and never once was able to get through it. It wasn't that he didn't know it, he was just so petrified with fear that he would dry at the end of every sentence and look helplessly at me, his eyes brimming over with tears.

After one night of this, I memorized his speech for him and fed it to him from the upstage corner of my mouth in a desperate bid to get the bloody play over.

The Kawartha Festival was one of the few summer stock theatres in Ontario that actually toured. After five days of rehearsal we would all get on an old bus, condemned years previously by some humanitarian school board but salvaged by the remarkable and enterprising Dennis Sweeting who put on a cap and switched his role from Producer to 'On-Tour Driver.' With a few pieces of the set, the costumes and some of the crew, the cast would all set out for Haliburton, a little town some sixty miles to the north of Lindsay. Dennis reassured us about any inadequacies we might be feeling apropos of the short rehearsal period by telling us that the people in Haliburton were delighted to have anyone go there and do anything at all. Never mind professional excellence or any such similar notion.

"Oh, by the way," said Dennis, "we play on the stage of the High School, and the proscenium arch is only twelve feet wide."

With that bit of information went any notion of concern over the blocking. When I actually saw the stage I realized that it was more a question of fighting for a space and delivering your lines in the proper sequence than anything else.

There were no such things as dressing rooms. We changed in the school corridors and made up in the public washrooms, which gave us a chance to butter up some of the audience before the show.

In actual fact, Dennis had been right about the audience. The packed auditorium laughed long and hard at all our antics and didn't seem to mind at all that there was hardly any set and only one or two pieces of furniture.

Halfway through the first act I thought that this wasn't going to be so bad after all! And then it happened. My leading lady, a beautiful, vivacious and keen redhead from Alberta, fresh out of drama school and doing her first professional engagement, hurled herself into her role with such enthusiasm that when she started her crying scene in the middle of the first act, she blew her nose so forcefully into her piece of kleenex that she occasioned a nosebleed. And I mean a nosebleed. It flowed like a river in spring.

"Must've been an artery," I thought. "Probably the main one to her brain!"

As she sat there on the one chair on stage, blood flowing everywhere, snorting her way through her narrative, I took one of the t-shirts from the basket of laundry and handed it to her. She certainly wasn't doing much good with that sodden piece of kleenex. She looked bizarre as she cried, sputtered, forgot where she was in her speech, mopped furiously with the laundry, threw her head back, rolled her eyes…it was a performance I shall never forget. The mosquitoes loved it! There had been a few mosquitoes at the opening of the show, but as word of the nosebleed spread quickly, the entire colony descended on us in droves, like vampires, biting and sucking to their hearts content.

On we went. I remember looking at one of the actors who was delivering a tirade at me, and was fascinated to see the drops of blood bursting though his greasepaint, and counted no less than seven bites before he concluded his speech.

By the end of the show, all of us were slapping at mosquitoes with such regularity we looked and sounded like a grade three rhythm band. The audience was apoplectic, doubled over with laughter. My leading lady's nosebleed abated but never quite stopped until we were back on the bus for Lindsay. We were exhausted from the ordeal.

'The Bat'

The second show I did that summer was an absolutely foul piece by Mary Roberts Rhinehart entitled 'The Bat'. I hadn't originally been scheduled, for this play, but whoever had been engaged couldn't come at the last moment. He probably read the script and cut his throat instead. In any event, I blithely agreed to play the role when Dennis offered it to me.

What a turkey! Two and a half hours of red herrings and every conceivable oddity in the way of characters that one could imagine, including a 'Chinaman' who was going to be played by the twelve year old kid.

After reading the script, I thought that the only way to have any fun with this piece was to play the characters like comic strip people. Indeed, the dialogue read as though it had been taken straight from that source. I played the detective like Fearless Fosdick, and it worked exceedingly well.

The largest role in the play, described in the script as an elderly patrician lady, was played by a much loved and respected elderly actress whom I liked on sight. She was an old trouper, had a great sense of humour and an undeniable presence and professionalism. Unfortunately, five days was not enough time for her to learn what proved to be a role longer than Hamlet. Consequently, every night was an adventure!

Once, when she and I were alone on stage, she went from page 32 to page 42 in the script. When she realized what she had done she looked helplessly at me and froze! I could hear a great scurrying from the actors backstage, wondering who should come on next. Barely able to remember my own part in this convoluted nightmare, I nevertheless undertook the job of summarizing ten pages of plot in what must have been one of the more memorable bits of invention of my career. It began with, "What you meant to say was…"

Dennis, both Producer and Director of this particular piece, told me later that he was standing at the back of the theatre and didn't think the audience noticed that anything was wrong. Aside from being kind, gentle, good humoured and a true lover of the theatre, Dennis is also an incurable optimist.

'Androcles and The Lion'

On the strength of my performance in 'The Bat,' I was hired for the following season, to play Dracula three times! I arrived at the lobby of the theatre and was delighted to find my friend Alison, a young actress of considerable talent who was in Lindsay for the entire season, and had been hired to appear in just about everything else but Dracula.

"Did you hear about our production of 'Androcles and The Lion'?" she asked, her bright eyes sparking with the anticipation of one eager to do it to me with a good theatre story.

"No," I replied, "but let's go sit down someplace and you can tell me."

Behind the theatre is a canal, beside which is a charming old ruin of a mill. We sat near it and Alison told me the following.

During the past winter, while adjudicating an amateur play festival, Dennis came across a production of 'Androcles and the Lion' which he felt would be just perfect for his upcoming summer season at Lindsay and hired neophyte director Simon Johnston to direct the play.

Simon was thrilled, as he'd never directed a play by George Bernard Shaw and went directly to work on the script. However, the version Dennis had seen was not by George Bernard Shaw; it was by someone else and had a cast of about eight people. The Shavian version had a cast of thousands, if you wanted to use that many Christians, gladiators, soldiers' etc.

When Simon arrived in Lindsay to pick up his directorial duties, imagine his surprise when he began to discuss casting with Dennis, the Producer.

Never one to miss the opportunity to turn misfortune into good fortune, Dennis said, "A Shaw play at the Kawartha Festival? Why not!" His eyes were bright and shiny with the prospect of bringing the classics to the people of Lindsay. In no time at all he was busily tendering names to the astounded Simon for his cast.

A group of young people from San Salvador was in Lindsay on some kind of theatre exchange program. They only spoke Spanish and had an interpreter with them. They could play the Christians! Veteran performer Jack Northmore, 6'2" tall, would be a riot as the lion. Handsome Robin Ward would be perfect as something else; the veterinarian's son Henry, only fifteen but huge, would be great as the head of the Romans; and so on and so on.

The final bit of genius was to cast the beautiful Alison as the head of the gladiators. She received a note to this effect the following day in the middle of a rehearsal for something else that was about to hit the boards, and arrived at the first rehearsal, ready to read the play.

The rehearsal hall was crowded with what must have been the largest cast ever to have been assembled for a Kawartha Theatre production. The San Salvadorians were particularly colourful, as their notion of action was to lie about and feel each other in some sort of tactile attempt to discover truth! The neophyte director was shouting at them as one does when you don't speak the language. But the San Salvadorians seemed content to continue rolling about the floor in a euphoric ecstasy of their own, kissing and hugging as they went, possibly the happiest group of Christians ever to have set foot in an arena.

Eventually the reading took place and the hapless, beautiful Alison, in the best baritone she could manage, read the part of the head of the gladiators.

At the conclusion of the reading, she picked her way through the tactile San Salvadorians, collared the frantic young director and said, "Simon, this just isn't going to work!"

"I realize that," said Simon, "you go and tell Dennis!"

She approached Dennis' office and very quietly told him that under no circumstances would she ever be able to bring off the role of head of the gladiators. Dennis leaned forward and said, "Nonsense Alison. You'll be wonderful as the head of the gladiators. I truly believe that this will be a wonderful stretch for you."

Alison realized she was dealing with a closed mind and smiled pleasantly and retreated quietly. Twenty minutes later, she simply told him that she was not playing the head of the gladiators in this or any other production and if it meant leaving town on the next bus she was prepared to do this. Eventually Simon convinced Dennis that this role had to be re-cast.

Reluctantly Dennis accepted the ultimatum and peevishly shot off to the bar and offered the role of head of the gladiators to the bartender, a loud burly gent who was delighted with the whole idea. Alison took the role of a beautiful wife of the Romans who had no lines but she got to wear a great costume and a lot of eye make-up.

By the time opening night came along, it seemed that half of the town was involved in the super gala production of George Bernard Shaw's 'Androcles and the Lion.'

The curtain went up on the Lindsay version of ancient Rome in a performance that was not without incident. Robin Ward's costume was a short leather skirt and a fishnet jacket which had unfortunately shrunk in the wash and looked like a training bra on his well-proportioned upper body.

The Salvadorians were still kissing and feeling each other as they marched from the back of the auditorium up on to the stage, happy as could be to face their death in the jaws of the lions. Their cue to enter was to have been given by Henry, the veterinarian's son, who, instead, was sitting this very moment in Jack Northmore's dressing room asking him what each particular stick of grease paint was used for.

There was a long delay on stage while someone went for Henry and eventually got him to the wings, where Henry came down with a severe case of stage fright and stood rooted to the spot.

Finally, someone else ran on to the stage and announced, "Here come the Christians!" These magic words having been spoken, the happy, kissing San Salvadorians did their march down the aisle. Several minutes later, after the Christians disappeared, Henry decided he wasn't frightened after all. He stepped out in the middle of the next scene, and in an incongruously high-pitched voice for the large body containing it, announced, "The Christians are coming!"

At this juncture, neophyte director Simon Johnston went backstage and tried to kill poor Henry, who was rather pleased with what he thought was a job well done. The stage manager had to physically restrain poor Simon, whose rage was indescribable and eventually threw him out the back door.

'Dracula'

Alison's story of 'Androcles and The Lion' left me paralyzed with fear for what might be ahead for me in 'Dracula.' 'Dracula' is a show that requires a piece of magic to happen every five minutes and at this point I didn't know who would be in it, or who the director was, except for his name. Twenty minutes later I met him in the theatre auditorium, jumping about in a pair of cut-off jeans. His head of curly brown hair, turned-up nose, and eager boyish enthusiasm belied his thirty years. His name was Tim Bond, the *enfant terrible* director. We introduced ourselves.

Tim outlined his plans for 'Dracula,' which included just about every theatrical trick I'd ever heard of, plus some new ones that no one had ever heard of. The play was going to be full of excitement from beginning to end; with a glorious flash finish that would include flaming torches, a ballet chase in the crypt, rats, bats, Bach's 'Toccata and Fugue in D,' a collapsible stake to actually nail the vampire into the staircase, a fog machine and lots and lots of blood.

By the time Tim finished describing all of this, I began to feel less tense, and had really picked up on his excitement over the piece.

The next day at the first read-through, I was very happy to see the young actress from the previous summer, the one with the nosebleed. She had been well chosen for the part of my victim Lucy. Her neck was so long, that at the end of the second act when Dracula actually sinks his fangs into it, her long neck, stretched back as it was, would cut off her windpipe and she'd invariably pass out as the curtain descended.

Fortunately, I'd been trained in my early life as a Red Cross Swimming and Water Safety Instructor and had learned to do mouth-to-mouth resuscitation. So, just about every night after the second curtain, I'd remove my fangs, revive the actress, and have lots of time to change and get ready for the third act.

As for her concerns… "nothing to worry about," said the director, slapping 'Lucy' on her backside. "David's a very responsible person!"

The intrepid pursuer of vampires, Dr. Van Helsing, was played by a huge, fat, comic whose face was a household image from having appeared on so many television commercials. He was a Lindsay favorite, and apparently had expressed a desire to play a serious role. As a result, a part that had become identified with slim, wiry, classical actor Peter Cushing was to be played by a three-hundred pound tub of lard with a face like a giant bloodhound! Nothing much could be done about that. He was a star in Lindsay.

The juvenile was played by a truly appalling little actor with a pot belly, large hips, doe eyes and an altogether middle-eastern look about him. The role of Jonathan Harker is an extremely difficult role, as he has the most improbable dialogue of any of the characters. In subsequent productions of this play some very good actors didn't handle the role very well. But in this, my first production, this actor managed to get laughs just about every time he opened his big mouth.

The rest of the cast were locals. I can't remember whether it was the dentist, the dogcatcher, or the restaurateur who played Lucy's father; and as far as the comic relief were concerned, I don't ever want to remember them again. The role of the demented, spider-eating maniac was played by a demented spider-eating maniac, a career I've not followed in later years with too much interest.

Rehearsals went along splendidly under the direction of our young terrier, Tim Bond, who showed remarkable directorial attributes. I was really working well under his watchful eye, and he did manage to do wonders with our motley group in the space of five days.

At the technical rehearsal, we hit our first major snag. Before the rehearsal began, Tim asked the technical director, "Where's the second act set?"

"What second act set?" came the last words that particular gentleman ever uttered in that theatre!

Somehow for opening night, a second act set miraculously appeared. I never knew how Tim got all that together, but he did get it and everything else together.

The curtain went up. The fat comic got a hand on his entrance, which infuriated me, but his struggle to come to real terms with vampire hunting didn't really pay off. The people who trusted him to make them laugh were disappointed. They really weren't interested in his attempts to be a serious actor. The juvenile, on the other hand, got loads of laughs, derisive though they were, just by opening his silly mouth.

In the second act, Dracula has a spectacular entrance though a pair of French doors. To achieve the effect of his flying through them, a trapeze was rigged backstage from which I would 'let go' at the last moment and seem to fly through them soundlessly and interrupt the puzzled Dr. Van Helsing. In the panic to erect the second act set, the balustrade outside the French doors still had some nails protruding from the upper railing, right smack in the middle of my flight pattern.

The moment came. I swung out on the trapeze, my full-length cape swirling behind me. At precisely the right moment I let go of the trapeze, swung though the French doors, my cape caught on the protruding nails and jerked me straight back through the doors and with a loud crash I landed on my arse, knocking over the balustrade as I fell.

As quickly as I could, I reappeared, mustering all the menace I could under the circumstances, to face the large, sweating Van Helsing who said his line, which, alas was… "I didn't hear you, Count."

The audience screeched! You would have had to be deaf as a post not to have heard that entrance. I'm sure the crash could have been heard in several neighboring towns.

Moments later, another bit of magic was to happen with a mirror. As everyone knows, vampires have no reflection in a mirror. Van Helsing notices this and remarks upon it, thereby enraging the caped count, who gestures to the mirror and it smashes mysteriously into many pieces.

To accomplish this bit of wizardry, a spring mechanism was devised to be released by one of the crew backstage at the same moment I made my gesture.

I don't trust mechanical devices of any kind as I don't really understand them and voiced this concern at rehearsals every time we got to this section. To pacify me, a brass vase was put on the set as a back-up precaution should the 'device' ever fail.

The moment came. I gestured, the mirror smiled happily back at me, or should I say, 'sneered', and remained unbroken. Not to be put off, I swirled upstage to the brass vase. As I picked it up I noticed that some idiot had stuffed a load of peacock feathers into it, just what was needed to foil my aim.

I shot the vase across the stage. It missed the mirror and went straight through the set. The audience's squeals of delight were tripled when I turned to them, supposedly regaining my composure and said, "Forgive me, I detest mirrors." At that moment, I really did!

Onward the play progressed to the big second act flash finish when Dracula creeps in the window and stealthily slides across the stage to the couch downstage center upon which lies the hapless Lucy. We looked forward to it so much, as we had thundering, heavy organ music accompanying the action and eerie fog seeping in the window and clinging to the velvet cape...when it worked properly. We really didn't have time to rehearse the lad on the fog machine and his last instructions before the play began were to "give it lots of fog!"

The moment came, the music started and so did the boy on the fog machine...pump, pump, pump, pump. I was standing next to him, counting slowly to ten as I was instructed. But by the time I got to eight, I was totally enveloped in fog. I started to move forward and could still hear the pump, pump, pump, pump of the machine.

By this time I couldn't see anything at all on stage. Even the few special lights that were on for the magic moment were of no help to guide me.

I wandered through the soup, whispering to the hapless Lucy, who was somewhere around, "where the hell are you?"

"Over here," came the reply.

I headed for the sound of her voice and fell over the back of the couch on top of her. Even from this unfortunate vantage point I couldn't see her. The boy was still pumping furiously outside the French doors. The audience could see nothing on stage and by this time the wall of fog was drifting towards them. The organ music blasted away, the fog kept coming and I was determined to see our charade through to the end.

I got Lucy to her feet in the middle of all this whiteout and was just about to sink my fangs into her neck when a hand reached out and grabbed me. It was the stage manager who had come on stage to tell us that the curtain was down. It was one of the few times that the long- necked actress didn't pass out, because we never got to finish that bit that night.

That intermission was especially long, as it took some time to clear the stage and the auditorium of the dreaded fog. But there was still the third act.

The third act had some wonderful effects planned. Many of them worked.

The sudden and almost miraculous disappearance of Dracula before the audience's eyes is surely one of the highlights of the show. It happens at that point in the play when it would seem that the fanged monster has been trapped and cornered by the pursuers.

Just when it looks like he's been captured, the juvenile, with a great scream emanating from him, rushes across the stage and hurls himself upon the tall breakaway velvet drapes to let in the sunlight, which any fool knows will destroy a vampire.

During this bit of what's called mis-direction, I simply had to duck behind the couch. It's split second timing and even people who later came to see the show again swore they never took their eyes off me and still imagined they'd seen me disappear before their very eyes.

However, on opening night of this production, at the precise moment, the juvenile rushed screaming across the stage and hurled himself upon the drapes. The seam that was supposed to break away had been basted too well and the drapes didn't give...but the set did. Set, drapes and all came tumbling down on top on poor Harker with a great wrenching rip, tear and crash. Talk about mis-direction! The rest of us on the other side of the stage could have sat down to a game of poker and no one would have paid the slightest attention to us. By this time, I would rather have been playing poker…anything other than what I was doing.

But we haven't finished. There's still the crypt scene, where the stake is finally plunged through the Count's heart. This was all to be done to Bach's 'Toccata and Fugue in D,' while the relentless pursuers, to the great concern of the Producer and in spite of his protests, were carrying flaming torches. Every precaution was taken to insure there would be no danger of fire. Everyone in the theatre business is terrified of fire.

At that magic moment when tubby Dr. Van Helsing is hammering the collapsible stake into the heart of Dracula, the juvenile, who was standing above me on the staircase, was so fascinated with the proceedings that he held his flaming torch just enough askew to set fire to the set. Fortunately, all that was left to do was for me to die, which I did in short order, and for the pursuers to bless themselves as the curtain descended.

The audience was spellbound as they watched this death scene being played against the now flaming set and screamed their approbation as the curtain descended.

The fire was put out quickly with the available extinguishers and the resultant smoke quickly filled the stage. The curtain was raised for our call and the audience cheered the group of players who could barely been seen, but who could be heard choking and coughing to a man. It was a night I shall never forget.

Believe it or not, 'Dracula' was a huge hit in Lindsay that summer and broke all previous box office records. The Director and I got so fond of the piece we even did four more productions of it, each one getting bigger and bigger. Years later, 'Dracula' had big revivals in New York, London and in the movies, but I wonder if any of those later productions enjoyed the fun we had with the old Count!

MISS FLEMING
AND THE BOMB

Miss Fleming was one of the first secretaries I ever had –
efficient, speedy, bright, and alive to all the skills of
her chosen profession of legal secretary. She dressed neatly
and in a business-like way, but always had a little extra bit of
something on her person which underlined her very
pronounced femininity. A scarf, a pin, a flower, and
sometimes just a tiny bit too much perfume reminded one
that Miss Fleming was enjoying being a girl. She was short,
red-headed, plump, curvaceous and only seventeen. I was
her first boss.

In 1962, she had been with me for about three months
when the morning of the Cuban missile crisis arrived. Both
Americans and Canadians were a little tense as to whether
or not it was the right time to run for shelter. At my office,
Miss Fleming, unbeknownst to me, was being quietly terrified
by the older secretaries in the cloakroom as to whether we'd
all live to see the day through or not. The newspaper headlines
that morning read 'By Eleven O'clock We Shall Know.'

When I arrived that morning, Miss Fleming brought my

mail in to me. I asked her to take some dictation straight away. After several abortive attempts, I asked her if anything was wrong. She looked pale, withdrawn and not her chirpy self at all. She hummed and hawed and fidgeted and assured me that she was all right. I tried a few more letters but it wasn't working. Something was wrong.

"Miss Fleming, you go type up what you have and I'll make a few calls." She left.

About five minutes later, while I was on the phone, I looked up to see a very worried and nervous Miss Fleming sitting across from me. She was nearly in tears.

At the end of my conversation, I hung up the phone, walked over and closed my office door and returned to my chair behind the desk.

"Now, there is something bothering you Miss Fleming, and I want you to feel perfectly free to tell me what it is. If there's anything I can do to help, be certain that I shall."

"Oh Mr. Brown," she started, "It's this international situation. Everyone told me when I came in for work this morning that we could all be dead by eleven o'clock. I'm so upset that my fingers won't hit the right keys, and I can't read my shorthand. I can hardly remember my own name!"

She was in a very sorry state, and I was sincerely moved to comfort her. I started: "Now Miss Fleming, I don't think it's really as bad as all that. And in any case, all you and I can do at this moment is to go about our work as best we can and hope that those in power will do their jobs as well as we do ours."

She rejoined: "Oh, but Mr. Brown, if the bomb comes, well…I haven't…you know…never! …not even once."

As the nickel dropped and I understood what it was she was really concerned about, the expression on my face must have been a study. I looked out the window for a moment and then turned back to her. As gently and as quietly as I could, I leaned across the desk, looked into her troubled blue eyes and said, "Don't worry Miss Fleming, I promise you, it'll be the last thing I do."

Her face lit up and she bounced to her feet and said, "Oh, thank you Mr. Brown," and scampered out of the office. Problem Solved!

A few minutes later her fingers were skipping over the typewriter keys. I sat looking out the window, waiting...waiting for the sound of the siren that never came!

HOSPITALITY
AND OLD SOCKS

In the autumn of 1975, I was working as an actor on tour with the Theatre New Brunswick production of 'Frankenstein.' It was a very happy time for me, made the more happy because of the success of the production and the warmth of the people of the Maritimes and Newfoundland. I'm from that area and was very proud when other members of the company were so complimentary about either the geography or the people, or both.

We toured every little town and city and even small villages of New Brunswick, P.E.I., Nova Scotia and Newfoundland. And though this is not a story about that tour, I will say that hospitality everywhere we went was unforgettable. Maritimers have a basic philosophy that the more you feed a person, the better off he or she is.

I was sitting in my brother's kitchen one morning when he appeared in his pyjamas, opened the refrigerator door, looked in for a long while, closed the door, looked at me, stretched out his arms and said, "There! Ya See! Last night there was a turkey, a ham and a roast beef and this morning there's nothing! That means everyone's eating and they're all well!" Then he disappeared, probably to get dressed and go to the nearest restaurant.

On this memorable tour, I was playing the role of Frankenstein's creature. To portray him, my face was painted a basic shade of blue and I wore nine-inch platform boots, concealed by a cleverly designed costume. The character never missed evoking enormous sympathy from the audience. After all, in his original state as Mary Shelley wrote him, he was a most pathetic and unfortunate case.

It was in Liverpool, Nova Scotia, after the show: a woman came to our company manager and said, "You tell dat big fella wit da blue face dat if he wants a good, hot, home-cooked meal, just come to da white hoose after da school-hoose on da way oot of town, an I'll fix him up."

I loved that woman for that offer which the company manager assured me was sincere and heartfelt.

Another simple gesture of hospitality happened after a show in New Glasgow. I had arranged for a certain lady and her nine children to be my guests at the performance, knowing that they very much wanted to come but couldn't possibly afford the tickets. I saw them after the show and was made to promise to stop at their home on our way out that night. We were racing off to North Sydney right after the show so that we'd be first in line for the ferry to Newfoundland the following morning. We did stop at her house and she pressed into my hands a brown paper bag which contained a superlative loaf of home-made bread, a square of butter, a piece of cheese and a bread knife.

Hours later, the five in our car were jammed into one really depressing motel room in North Sydney and wolfed down the simple offering as though it were a Roman banquet. I can't remember anything ever tasting better.

The reason for rushing off to North Sydney immediately after the show was to be first in line for the ferry to Port Aux Basques, which left very early in the morning. We'd been warned by some mine of misinformation that if you weren't in line early enough, you often had to wait most of the day on the pier for the next ferry, which didn't leave until late in the afternoon. We turned out to be the first in line. After a scant two hours sleep and a thoroughly miserable night, we were the only ones in line!

The rest of the company had sensibly gone to a pleasant hotel in New Glasgow, had a good night's sleep and an early morning drive which brought them to the ferry about ten minutes before it left. So much for the cleverness of car number one!

One word of caution to those of you who like a cocktail on the boat: beware the bartenders on that ferry! One of our troupe was complaining of sea-sickness and for some reason or other he asked me what he should do about it.

"A stinger on the rocks!" I said, "As many as you can get into you!" I didn't know if this would cure his sea-sickness or not, but I knew if he had enough of them, he wouldn't care about it.

We placed our order and I was psyching him up for this delicious concoction of brandy and white crème de menthe with tales of great evenings I'd had on this diet, when the drinks arrived. God, they were awful! The bartender said that he'd done what the book on cocktails had said. "Couldn't have," I protested.

It turned out that he didn't have any normal brandy so he used apricot; and since there was no white crème de menthe, he'd used green. I decided on scotch and water and my poor friend took quickly to bed and stayed there until we were steady at the dock in Port Aux Basques.

This was the first time I was ever in Newfoundland and I

was excited as could be because we were playing every city or town on the main highway. Pity it had to be December. The driving on some of those days was mind-boggling, but as it turned out, we only had to cancel one engagement because of fierce weather. All the good and humorous things they say about Newfoundlanders are true. Where else in the country do you find such an indigenous sense of humour? Have you ever heard of an Albertan sense of humour? Or the Ontario sense of humour?

The laugh quotient of our troupe went skyrocketing off the graph all through the Newfoundland tour, but one of the things I'll never forget was the phone-in show from St. John's. It was called the Ron Pomphrey show, and though phone-in shows are not my bag at all, when I accidentally stumbled upon this one, I became addicted.

One of the things that struck me was the fact that, unlike any other phone-in show I've heard, the people phoning in were very well-informed about the particular area of interest. On the political scene, they seemed to know an enormous amount about not only provincial politics and legislation, but federal as well.

The show was very cleverly designed so that someone phoning in from one of the outports with a grievance about his representation in Ottawa could be linked up by phone to that member in Ottawa. And believe me, there were some salient questions being asked of those members. This was participatory Democracy! Here it was truly happening in Newfoundland.

Many times, people phoned in just to give their opinion on some aspect of life that took their interest that morning. It wouldn't relate in any way to the question of the day or what the program was supposed to be directed towards, but nevertheless, Ron Pomphrey would give them the floor.

One such call came from a woman in Portugal Cove who

had the following to say: "Mr. Pomphrey, I jist wants to say a few words about the vegetables. Dey ain't flavor to dey anymore. De carrots an de turnips an da cabbidge, why man, dey all tastc de same. Dere was a toime when I'd make me corned beef an cabbidge and youse could smell it all over de Cove, but now win I makes it, yez has gotta stick yer nose roight inta da pot to smell anyting, an even den, alls ya kin smell is de bacon fat!"

Mr. Pomphrey, contemplatively: "I see..."

"Now, Mr. Pomphrey, I jist wants to say dis, I tinks its da chimicals, Mr. Pomphrey. I do. Dey're puttin' too much of da chimicals inta de soil. An Oi tinks dat if dey'd go back to de ol' fashioned meyjore dey'd be better off. Tank you." And she hung up.

And who could argue with her. She said it so colourfully and simply that I'll remember the lesson far longer than I would on reading a Royal Commission on the subject.

Oftentimes the show was used by people in remote parts of the island to get messages to others. Once, there was an ultimatum being delivered: "Mr. Pomphrey, dis is Agnes Grant and I looks after de golf course at such an such. Now someone, Mr. Pomphrey, has left four horses on fairway number noine, an dey been grazin' der for two days. Now Mr. Pomphrey, if dey ain't off dat course by dis Friday, an Oi hope de owner is listenin' ta dis, Oi'm callin' de S.P.C.A., an dey'll come an take dem away. An dat's dat!" She meant business. You could tell from the tone of her voice!

Some people phoned up just to be pleasant. I remember a call from Sister Agnes Marie, retired nun. She wanted to tell the listeners, since it was coming on to Christmas, about an incident that happened to her forty years before, when she was the prefect in a dormitory for twelve wayward girls.

"We were very poor," she said, "and couldn't afford any ornaments for the Christmas tree and on Christmas Eve I told the girls the story of the nativity. That night, when it came time to turn out the lights, the girls begged me to keep the door ajar. All night I could hear their little feet coming in and out of my room and in the morning, I saw on the Christmas tree twelve pieces of paper that said, "we love you, baby Jesus."

The interviewer thanked her for phoning in with a story that truly communicated the meaning of Christmas. He asked her if, before hanging up, she could sing a chorus from 'Silent Night'!

"Oh, I couldn't," said the old nun.

"Oh, come on," said Pomphrey.

"Well, I will if you'll sing it with me," said Sister.

Pomphrey was on the spot and had no choice but to agree. The two of them ground their way through a chorus of 'Silent Night,' the old nun remembering half the lyrics and Pomphrey, more or less, half the tune. Mercifully, they stopped after one chorus. He thanked her and took the next call.

"Is dat you Ron Pomphrey?" asked a raspy, crusty, deep voice.

"Yes, who is this calling please?"

"Dis is Arnold Tanner, from Bull's Bay," he replied.

"Yes Mr. Tanner, and what can I do for you this morning?"

"Oi wants to know if yez gaht eny old socks down der."

"Old socks...old socks?" said Pomphrey, "Why, did you want to use the wool to hook rugs or something like that?"

"No," said Mr. Tanner, "Oi jist wants some old socks to shove down de troat of dat old nun who was singin' Soilent Noight."

"Very nice," replied Pomphrey, slamming down the receiver.

I listened to the show every morning as we moved from

one place to another, ending up with a week in St. John's; and didn't I end up on the show myself to promote the 'Frankenstein' production! There was another guest on the show that morning. He was telling how to go about hunting the wild bologna of Newfoundland. According to him, the wild bologna looks much like the domestic variety save for two little slitty eyes, a long single hair down his back and four tiny feet. They supposedly live in holes in the mountain and if you make a noise like a moose, they stick out their heads, and all you have to do is grab them.

I'm very fond of almost everything bizarre and told this fellow how much I'd enjoyed his narrative. He was somewhat shy, but we hadn't been talking very long before he said, "If you don't care what ya eat, you and yer friends could come home to dinner."

THE HAT

It was on the first warm evening of the summer of 1973 when I first met Lillie Pope. A few friends had been to my second floor apartment in Rosedale for the evening and had left around one-thirty in the morning. I was picking up the empties and yawning when the buzzer sounded, indicating that someone was in the downstairs porch. I pressed the release button and quickly went to the balcony to see whose car might be out front. It was late, but perhaps one of my friends had left something behind.

I arrived on the balcony just in time to see a naked man darting across the street and into the bushes of the backyard of the house opposite mine. He wasn't very tall, had black, slightly kinky hair, a sinewy body, and best of all, black pointy-toed shoes with pale blue ankle socks. That's all I can tell you of him because his back was to me.

I yelled something like, "Far out man!" but he was moving steadily and quickly away from me, and I doubt that he heard me.

Meanwhile, up the stairs and falling into my arms, looking quite red in the face and bedraggled in the hair department, came two mature ladies. One was quite thin with frizzy, salt and pepper hair, a sallow complexion and tortoise-shell glasses. The other one was blonde, plump, had really perky features and beautiful white, even teeth.

The blonde introduced herself as Lillie Pope and was quick to tell me that she and her friend had just had the most horrendous experience.

"I'll bet!" I mused to myself.

It seems that Lillie and her friend Dot, who was visiting from Kamloops, had decided to have a late night walk around the crescent before retiring. Halfway through the walk, the naked runner jumped out of the bushes and waved his member at them.

Lillie had said to her friend, "Don't panic Dot, stay calm," and then proceeded to break into a gallop, leaving the confused Dot a few yards behind before she got the message.

The three of them – Lillie, Dot, and the naked runner – continued round the crescent at breakneck speed until they saw my lights, did a left turn and found refuge in my porch downstairs, which is enclosed by two glass doors. The naked runner stood outside the outer glass door, jumping up and down, shaking his member at them in glee while Lillie rang all the buzzers on the wall. It was then that my signal from upstairs released the lock on the inner door downstairs.

I asked her what he'd looked like. Lillie looked at me like I was demented and said "I didn't see his face!" I gave both ladies large brandies, some sympathy and later walked them home, looking all around as we went for a last glimpse of the runner.

After that, I only saw Lillie from time to time; and we'd nod politely to each other as we'd pass on the street. I learned from a mutual friend that she was much beloved in the neighborhood, was very eccentric, mother of three teenagers and a widow. She spoke a few languages, including Spanish and was independently wealthy, though not by any standards rich.

She had been invited to a dress-up Halloween party last year and consulted my friend as to what she should wear. My friend very sensibly suggested that whatever she wore, she should feel comfortable in it and also attractive. In fact, she suggested to Lillie that she'd make a perfect Spanish Senorita and would even lend her a black, wide-brimmed Spanish hat, the type so often worn by Spanish dancers. Lillie took one look at herself in the hat and was sold on the idea. She looked very beguiling in that black hat with her blonde hair, saucy blue eyes and those white, even teeth. And she knew it.

Months passed. My friend wondered about the hat and asked Lillie if she was through with it. With deep apologies Lillie told her the following: she had kept the hat because, as she told my friend, the most wonderful things happened to her when she wore it. Not only was she the hit of the Halloween party, with compliments from all the ladies and very real passes from all the gents, but it turned her date onto the point of a Black-Magic frenzy when they got home.

There were other little incidents of joy and elation that occurred to Lillie, and always when she was wearing the hat; so is it any wonder that she was reluctant to give it back to its rightful owner. But the best of all was yet to come.

One day, wearing the hat at her usual saucy angle, she was sitting in the subway and as happens in subways, became aware of someone staring at her. A quick, all-seeing glance in the direction of the stare revealed a handsome, swarthy, tall, Latin gentleman who was indeed staring at Lillie in the open, shameless way that Latin men seem to get away with when they're evincing signs of being in heat. This look at *el*

Latino produced a slight flush in Lillie's cheeks and she fiddled with the black cord that dangled from the brim of her hat.

The train shuffled through station after station until, at last, Lillie's station approached. She got up, aware that the Latin gentleman was still staring. But wait – he was getting up too!

"Is he going to follow me?" she thought, "What if he's one of those crazies." (Remember: this woman was chased around the crescent by a naked nut shaking his parts at her.)

She hastened through the station. Just when she reached the sidewalk, she heard him speak.

"Excuse me, I don't usually behave in such a forward manner, but it is your hat! It reminds me of Spain, my home. Please forgive me, but I don't know anyone here and wondered if you would have coffee with me."

Lillie's knees were like jelly and she was worried that the legs might let her down completely. He was so very polite and his voice was like a guitar concerto. He was also very handsome.

"Certainly not," said Lillie, turning on her heel and marching up the street, obeying some weird code that was instigated by Queen Victoria and drilled into ladies like Lillie from the time they were able to breathe.

All the way home she could have kicked herself. Why did she say no? After all, what harm would there have been to have a lousy cup of coffee with the guy. He was well dressed. He was polite. Maybe he doesn't know anyone in town. And he was so handsome.

A few weeks later, by God, didn't the same meeting happen again. Lillie couldn't believe her eyes when she sat down on the subway train and there, across the aisle, was the Latin gentleman. He smiled and, God love her, she smiled back (and Lillie's smile is a treat). She made a decision there and then. When they got off at the station they were both bound for, he living in the same neighborhood as she, she didn't decline his offer for coffee, but simply reached up, adjusted the angle of the hat to an even more provocative rake and took his arm.

For weeks they had a blissfully contented affair. He was a scientist working for the Spanish government on something having to do with feeding the third world from the ocean and she was just delighted and delightful. They did all the things you read about in the fantasy romance books – dancing, dining, walks, movies, theatre, concerts and very often just spending endless hours in each other's arms. And all the while, Lillie wore the hat. He loved it, and for her, it was her talisman. It brought them together and she'd wear it every day, just to keep the spell going.

However, it was only a temporary posting. The Latin gentleman eventually had to go back to Spain. It was something they both knew they were going to have to face, but like young people looking at death, you know it's coming, but you really don't think it will ever happen to you. Eventually, he did leave, and it was sad.

The day after he left, Lillie went to the Kensington market to do her Saturday morning shopping. As she rounded a corner, the wind lifted the hat off her head and blew it away. She searched the market for most of the day. She talked to shopkeepers, customers and children – anyone who'd listen to her. She offered a $25 reward. But it was gone and never seen again.

The day after I heard this story, I was on the subway and who should I see but Lillie. It was very cold and I was struck dumb at the sight of Lillie's hat – a huge black fur Russian Tartar's hat, complete with a peak towering up out of the fur. I walked up the street with Lillie, chattering about this and that, but the whole time we were chatting I kept wanting to say, "Lillie, I love your hat. Would you let me take you for a cup of coffee?"

LETTERS

LETTERS TO ED STEPHENSON

Edmonton

Dear Ed:

Thanks for your latest missive. I love the Sam Pepys style you've adopted to get as much information across as possible. Had a letter from Rita this a.m. which is so different. As you might expect, she has the ability to spin a yarn about an afternoon in the garden with Kitty and Decker into a Neo Jane Austen idyll!

Yesterday, there were twenty-four family members here to have a mass-utilitarian, all purpose, once-a-year birthday celebration. This was prompted by the fact that J & T are away so much, they miss everyone's birthday. Most of them were given $800 natural gas barbecues. I thought that was taking their guilt feelings a little seriously. I went with them on the shopping expedition and argued for the $99 models, but no one ever listens to me!

Lynn was there with her spawn and the Spawnor. At one point I found myself uncharacteristically sitting with Ryley on my lap. He's seven months old. I gave him his first Slurpee. Grape flavored. You suck it out of plastic tube. His face was a study as he discovered this new flavor sensation. So differentfrom mother's milk. His little tongue was like a rotor blade on a high-speed helicopter. His eyes were sparkling. His baldness gives him a Benito Mussolini appearance and his ears, unfortunately... yes... Dumbo! Quite something when it's all in motion and hit up with a grape Slurpee. I fear he has his Uncle's taste for rum and water, however. How much of a taste I'll never know because I was caught and little Benito was handed over to someone else.

The style of the party itself was somewhat western mixed with Italian. The long table in the parking lot with the orange rented chairs gave it a definite Italian look when coupled with the hundreds of colored lights strung up overhead. The food was certainly western and so were the outfits everyone wore.

The surprise gift of the day was a present to J & T of a family portrait, which was taken between 6:00 and 6:45. Josie (the Rottweiler), Larry (Ann Margaret's boyfriend), Alysia (Larry's three year old daughter by his first marriage) and myself were not included in the group, not being immediate family. I argued that the Spawnor should not be included either, since he's not in fact married to my niece. But it was argued what the only reason he's not married to Lynn is that Lynn doesn't want to get married! Somehow or other, this got poor Lance into the picture. And besides, who was going to hold Benito, who by this time was definitely showing signs of not being able to hold his rum!

The wildlife here consists mostly of two dogs, many songbirds, packs of marauding coyotes, squirrels, barn cats, hummingbirds and some recently discovered frogs. Our dog Josie, the Rottweiler, has fallen in love with me. We go for long walks through the alfalfa. I marvel at the white puffy clouds, the green fields, the tall poplars and birches, the lake in the distance and the vast horizon. Josie is more taken with mysterious smells and aromas to which I am not privy. It was through Josie that I discovered the frogs, when she stopped at the lake for a dip and a slurp.

The songbirds are amazing. So many varieties and colours. A new fellow appeared the other day, identified as a Ruby Breasted Grosbeak. As there are no crows or magpies about, the songbirds proliferate.

Trevor and I will be going to Yellowknife on June 28th for a few days. It would appear that most of what we have to do can be done with very little time spent in Yellowknife itself.

In the meantime, Trevor keeps threatening new projects involving all sorts of unexpected things. I actually went to the Public Library two weeks ago, researched and finally put together for him a Purchase of Shares Agreement, which ended up being quite a heady document. No laughs however. It all had to do with an emerging electronics company.

Now he's hinting that I should take on managing directorship of this company. And if not that, then how about managing a Second Mortgage company for him, as there appears to be no satisfactory Second Mortgage company in Edmonton at this moment. These ideas have not been attractive, but he keeps coming up with them. One of them sounds good, but more of that if and when, over the months, it takes any shape.

The Edmonton Bridge Club continues to be a never-ending source of irritation and amusement. In addition to previously described oddballs, there has appeared, what I'm certain is a transsexual. God just couldn't have created all this. And I'm told she's living in sin with the pudgy man who accompanies her. Fancy that!

The best part is that I've found a really good player in Lorraine Macdonald. We've played three times together with the toughest groups, and though we've only come third, I think we might be 'contenders' when we get to understand each other's bidding a little better. She teaches bridge, so it's probably up to me to embrace things like negative doubles!

I'm still steeped in Wilbur Smith's amazing adventures. I've managed to collect just about everything he's written save three and I'm about half way through the entire output. Such colour! Such movement! Such breathtaking, stories and adventures.

I heard on the radio the other day that they've discovered huge gold finds in northeastern Alberta, ounces to the ton. Doesn't sound like much to me, but apparently this is one of the richest finds ever. I'm working on Trevor, who, every time I bring up the subject, gets this far-away look in his eye and in front of me, appears to shed forty years! Maybe, just maybe! Or is it too much Wilbur Smith?

Poul and Solveig are Danes who emigrated from Denmark forty years ago, and I suspect, are true Canadians. As a boy, he dreamed of coming to Canada to be a cowboy and that's pretty much what he's done. They invited us to their 'Pig Party' to celebrate Canada's birthday on July 1st. This is an annual event and I believe this last anniversary marked their 20th party. Their 'spread' lies about an hour west of Edmonton's city limits amid some very pretty rolling hills. On their acreage is the trailer they first used to weekend on this property. It's a reminder of where they came from, I suppose, because now they have an indoor pavilion, an outdoor pavilion, a swimming pool, a large ranch house and large houses for their three married children, B., Perri and the exotic-looking and very pregnant Tina. Horses and gardens complete the picturesque setting.

The party was large. Everything from babes in the womb to doddering elders. The food was ranch-style, featuring baked beans, potatoes baked and fried, coleslaw in vats, a couple of medium sized barbequed pigs and tons of other stuff.

Aside from the swimming, horseback riding, western style dancing and singing to the twanging of steel guitars, the main featured event – the most important 'test' of the celebration, the center of attention – was the horseshoe competition. It was already underway when we arrived at 3:00 P.M. and continued until 11:30 that night. I was forced into the game, protesting loudly that I'd never 'thrown a shoe,' but as luck would have it, I didn't disgrace myself and even made it to the semi-finals together with my partner Trevor, who again, fortunately, has extra long arms.

We were doing nicely until we were knocked off the course by two spotted early teens. Every time young Normie was up, I clinked my horseshoes and told him he was a rotten kid and would never amount to anything. In spite of that, they nosed us out with what I thought was more luck than skill and in my best stroke of bad sportsmanship, I let them know it.

The tournament continued until about 8:00 p.m. at which time I was hangin' out at the outside pavilion, knocking back some Lemon Hart. Suddenly Perri ambled up to his brother B., and he muttered, "Ah think hit's tahm ta tayke these turkeys, Bro."

B. didn't say anything. He just looked up towards the horseshoe situation and nodded slowly. Then in one quick move, he knocked back a large rum and coke.

The two of them slowly advanced toward the course and as they were moving, from out of nowhere, two other dudes were heading in the same direction. These men are about 35 to 40 years of age and three of them were straight out of Marlboro ads. The fourth one was too pudgy for Marlboro, but he cut quite a figure nonetheless, particularly with the vivacious Brenda hanging on his arm and showering him with kisses of encouragement.

These men looked lean and mean, all four of them wearing those moustaches that grow over the lower lip so that you can't tell if they're smiling or scowling. They all wore ten gallon hats, tight fitting jeans, shirts, jackets, neckerchiefs. And cowboy boots made from some exotic hide of some exotic creature that never heard of Canada nor cowboys nor boots! The brothers were blonde and had pale blue eyes. The competition had dark hair, and dark eyes. All four were drunk! All four moved slowly, and the concentration was fierce. None of the spectators made a sound except to ooh and aah at the expert tosses.

The game is won when one of the teams reaches 11. Before too long, the score was 9 to 8 for the dark-haired guys. Brother Perri was up. Uncharacteristically, brother B. suddenly broke into a little western jig and exclaimed, "We're gonna win cause that's mah Bro."

Perri adjusted his bowed legs as his pale blue eyes seemed to burn down the course. He held the shoe out in front of him for the longest time, waited and waited and waited. Not a sound anywhere. His armed dropped, one step forward into a semi stoop, the arm came forward, the shoe was released, it soared in a graceful arch, slowly spun and finally clipped itself around the post with a resounding clank. Three points and the win. Expressionless, the four men shook hands and returned slowly to the bar, as if nothing happened. But you knew it did. The testosterone level at that party was high.

Yellowknife

The flight from Edmonton to Yellowknife takes about three hours if you make brief stops in Fort Smith and Hay River. The dragonflies at the airport in F.S. were the largest I've ever seen. Like little tugboats, they accompanied us down the runway. I could see them very clearly through my window.

In the little airport itself, which looked very northern Canadian, in blue, there was a display cabinet showing examples of beadwork moccasins and an instruction manual on how to work and weave porcupine quills. There were other things too, but that was really all that took my attention.

You'll be glad to know that the airport has all the necessary washrooms, ticket counters and in-and-out doors. I passed on Hay River and only the occasional look out at Great Slave Lake distracted me from my Wilbur Smith novel. G.S.L. is very muddy, by the way. And very large. And then Yellowknife, 'Gateway to the North.'

We were there for three days and we worked for most of that time, but did take a few hours here and there to case the joints. At either end of town there's a gold mine. In between there are a lot of newish looking buildings where the 17,000 people huddle together, except for the Dene (pronounced Denny) Indians, who live in a section called Latham Island. We went to this island and after we crossed over the bridge we were stopped at a check point by two young people who wanted to know if we had any liquor in the car because there was a three day moratorium on liquor on Latham Island. (Later, however, in a telephone conversation with a fish restaurant on Latham Island, we were assured that there would be no problem getting a drink if we wanted one!)

I was told that due to the land settlements and whatever, the Dene Indians were a very wealthy tribe. There wasn't a lot of wealthy ostentation though. Other than the simple habitations, the only thing that stuck out was what looked like a white man's club, already showing signs of decline in spite of the piece of cardboard in the window upon which had been written: 'Remove Your Shoes.'

Another section of Ycllowknife that took my notice was a rather prettily located Granola People colony, situated on the water and built in the most imaginative shapes, practically on top of each other. One can easily visualize the winter nights being passed, endlessly, in rollicking sing-a-longs and drinking of spruce-flavored mulled wine. I swear I could hear the strains of 'On top of Old Smokcy' as we meandered through the twisting lanes.

A number of seaplanes were moored at piers and, of course, numbers of motor boats. And just off shore were a dozen or so colorfully painted houseboats. Every morning the excrement from the houseboats is boated across to the mainland for disposal in something called the Honey Wagon. I'm told there are inspectors who come around from time to time to make sure you're doing this. (I wonder if anyone secretly slips a bucket of shit into the lake?)

Most people though, if they aren't living in an apartment building, are living in a trailer. They are two types – single or double. The former sell for about $137,000 the latter $185,000. Things are expensive in Y.K.; but don't forget, the government gives you a living allowance just for being there.

There are a couple of high rises (10-12 stories) and there are many government buildings. The government buildings are designer originals, the most conspicuous of which are the Prince of Wales Northern Heritage Building and the N.W.T. Administration Building. Next time I go to Y.K. I shall find out what goes on in there. At the moment, I'm afraid I already know. There are many, many other civil service buildings, as well as skating and curling rinks, swimming pools, tennis courts. In fact, just about every recreational facility you can imagine.

The terrain is forbidding. It consists of two elements: very hard looking rock and stunted trees. Where these two elements are framed by water, I suppose one might allow a certain beauty. Personally, I find sand and palm trees more effective. There really isn't much more to say about the terrain. Yellowknife at night really doesn't exist at this time of year because the sun goes down at 11:30 p.m. and is up again at 12:30 a.m.

Our first night, we ate downtown at the Chinese café. While we were waiting for the order to be filled, a man came in from the street holding a bottle of ketchup. He shouted to the owner, "Hey, someone left this on the sidewalk!" and put it on the counter. Two Indian girls came in and ordered fifty dollars worth of fried stuff. Three more Indians came in and sat at the next table. One of them was about 30 years old, exuded electric energies from every pore, had long, flowing black hair and wildness in his eyes that was startling to see. Of the three, he was the only one who ate. The woman had a huge face, most of her teeth and was…well, let's call her 'zoftic.' She smoked Export A cigarettes the whole time. The third one could have been anyone…or dead for that matter. Not a word was spoken by any of them. They were still there when we left. Hell, it was a Tuesday night. I'll bet on Saturday night it's a lot different.

Anyway, enough of Yellowknife except to say this: The mines employ about six hundred people. Except for the spin-off merchants that would naturally evolve in a small community, the rest are civil servants and Indians. They get a pay-cheque every week from the government. They're all happy. They're all laughing. And why not? The government is pouring two billion dollars a year into this completely artificial creation, which, if it were erased from the maps, would be no loss to anyone or anything. Our taxes are going into perpetuating a completely artificial and unnecessary town called Yellowknife. It really pisses me off.

And by the way, I looked into staking claims while I was there. You know of course that diamonds have been discovered in the area. Behind every rock there's someone with a stake and hammer. So far, in the Yellowknife area alone, they have staked an area larger than New Brunswick. I don't mind all of that. That's all to the good. But what the civil service is doing there en masse, stroking the Denes or what ever they do, as I say, is irritating in the extreme.

We may or may not have to return.

LETTERS TO LYNN

May 1985

Dear Lynn:

This letter is entitled "Day two of the Scarsdale." It's not even nine o'clock and I'm writing letters, having had my morning ration of whatever it was that killed Dr. Tarnover, my mind torn between concentrating on this letter and lunch.

This is really necessary because ever since I had hepatitis, I've had this gargantuan appetite, which for a good three months manifested itself in such adventures into foodland that my naked profile looked like one of those Ethiopian famine victims at the distended belly stage.

The ten weeks in Halifax were like a shot in the arm both professionally and socially. I've always been shy of doing Shakespeare and had to come to terms with that by playing Toby Belch in 'Twelfth Night.' It not only was great fun to do, but John Neville came to see the last performance and was extremely complimentary about my work. He also indicated to Ed Stephenson a few weeks later that he'd be offering me a contract at Stratford in '86. Whether he does or not remains to be seen, but in the meantime, it's been a boost to my sometimes flagging morale.

Another first in Halifax was my first attempt at a kid's show. I played a pirate captain in a piece called 'The Mystery of Oak Island' that was fun. Pirate acting for ten- year-olds can be very invigorating.

One night, Uncle Donald's 12, 10 and 8 year olds came to the six o'clock show and afterwards I took them to the Bistro for dinner and then to the Silver Spoon for dessert. We had a great time.

The evening got off to an inauspicious start when, confronted by an almost totally French menu, I panicked and started to do a lot of talking about what they should eat. The three of them were brushed, combed and shinily scrubbed. They sat there stating at me, listening to me running off at the mouth. Eventually when I paused for breath, the ten year old said, "Uncle David, You sound just like nana."

I got the message and we then settled down to a quite riotous four hours of merriment. I told them a lot of family secrets about their father and Uncle Brownie from when they were kids and they in turn poured out a lot of their little indiscretions. My favorite was the ten year old's recounting how he, when he put up his hand to go to the washroom, he didn't always go to the washroom.

"Where do you go?" I asked.

"Sometimes I go to the coatroom and throw all of the coats on the floor," he replied. This struck me as being very interesting!

Much love,
Uncie

November 1986

Dear Lynn:

I found these ugly Xmas cards in a box of things to be thrown away and since I don't have any writing paper, I'm going to use these up.

Thanks a lot for the 'Uncle Ethel.' That really set me up for the week! However, since returning home from Stratford, I've lost seven pounds and haven't had a cigarette!!!

My energy quotient has gone up significantly. I get up at 8 a.m. and do things like wash walls, floors, vacuum, laundromat, write letters, etc. etc. I race around the city on foot – not subway.

Good news! Genni and Jeffrey have invited us to Newcastle for Xmas. Means we don't have to buy a fucking Xmas tree!
When are you arriving – so I can plan things!
Must run. Have to wash all the shelves

Uncie

Camp Stratford
Springtime

Dear Lynnsy Poops:

Your St. Patrick's Day card was positively pubic and your letter was too good for me to put off writing for another minute.

Your letter, by the by, raises the question as to whether your boyfriend Ron's sanity may not be in jeopardy. Is he really equipped to play 'All Out War?' He seems much too sensitive and honest to me, but I'm sure you know what you are doing. Just remember that 75 per cent of known axe murderers were very gentle people who claimed "they were pushed."

Things are much the same at 122 Queen Street except the kitchen's been painted, the nun's cell has been wall-papered and the Portuguese lace curtains have been replaced with American Gigolo-type venetian blinds.

Roberta's father, Robert, is a year older and badly in need of a haircut. He has scarcely been out of the house for five months, so that's not surprising. When I arrived, I told him at 1 p.m. it was time for him to be up and doing. (Doing what I don't know). He said, "I'm getting up in an hour and I have a project. I'm going to go through every pocket I have and see if I can't find my teeth."

Dumb a question as it was, I asked "how long have they been missing?"

"They've been missing ever since I flushed my wristwatch down the toilet," he said.

I've been gorging ever since I got here, and finally broke 190 yesterday. Disaster! The only thing that will fit me is the sweater you knit for me. Everyone still raves about it by the way. Except for that 'pinch faced' little Kim Horseman who muttered something about 'pregnant' the other day. Little bitch!

I've been to the superstore every day taking advantage of the many sales. Every time I go through those doors, I feel like Dom Deluise going into a refrigerator. At the moment I have in the freezer downstairs, for your visit, two ducks, a goose, a leg of lamb, three mutilated turkeys, two stewing hens, two roasting chickens, cakes, pies and ice cream. So maybe you had better come for a longer visit this time.

I'm only rehearsing 'Three Sisters' at the moment , but I'm loving the role. It's the best part I've had in four seasons. Such a splendid play! I think the cast is excellent and Neville's been in the best form I've ever known him to be. Have you seen his film? 'Baron Munchausen?' Apparently he's stupendous.

I'll phone your mother on Easter Sunday. Wonder how much damage she did in San Francisco?

Love Ya

Uncie

November 1987

Dear Poo Poo:

Thanks for the itinerary plus enclosures. Interesting juxtaposition of your mother and Dear Abby!

Loved the article on computerized Shakespeare. Must admit, when I have to memorize it, it could be said simpler!

Today I started off as usual. Dieting. Ate some fruit salad which is supposed to do until suppertime. But I never got by Alfred's Fish and Chips at around 1:30. I covered every centimeter of it in ketchup...and washed the whole greasy mess down with...ready?...a diet Coke.

The income tax audit continues. Round one began in an 'examining room' in a government building on Adelaide St., the interior of which puts one in mind of a federal penitentiary.

My inquisitor is a Greek gentleman called Mr. Batsos, or, as he would have it known, Meeshahrr Baahhtchosshh. He looks like an aged, moulting gerbil and every time I glare at him, I see a bloodsucking pickpocket, who is about to strip me of every last nickel I own.

His English is so bad that I make the son of a bitch repeat everything at least four times... sometimes five. I figure I can go pretty far with him because there's a big sign outside of the elevator that says I'm entitled to be treated with respect.

In a feeble and not well calculated attempt to put me at ease, he said, in his pathetic tongue, that he had audited many actors before and would understand if I were nervous. I stood up and, leaning across his desk, shouted at him, "I'm not nervous Mr. Batsos, I'm hysterical. Do you understand the meaning of the word hysterical?" The interview concluded shortly after that outburst.

Round two has just concluded with me delivering to him today a nine page letter with so many names, addresses and cross-references, that it will make him think twice about becoming a Canadian citizen before this is over.

Went to the doctor for a check up. Everything was going along just swell until he started talking about a proscopathy or words to that effect. He gave me this little kit with three sushi skewers…the front end of the stool…and the back end of it. I can't tell you the images that sprang into my head…and the ridiculousness of it all, not to mention the revulsion. One would have to be a contortionist, acrobatic and fairly proficient at juggling to get all that together as I saw it. And, if that weren't bad enough, he wanted me to take this suppository two hours prior to my next visit. And this was to clean me out in about an hour. When I got to his office, I was then expected to 'dump' again. Well, I told him that this was simply out of the question, that I was emotionally completely unprepared for any such carry on and would be quite content to leave the mysteries of my lower bowel, just that…a mystery!

I'm really looking forward to your visit. I know it will be fun without having to plan a lot of stuff. There are oceans of things to do and see…not to mention shopping. There are great stores everywhere.

Much Love,
Uncie

LETTER TO ALEXANDER

March 9, 1999

Dear Alexander:

Many thanks for your newsy and pensive letter, which I've read and enjoyed many times. It would appear that your time in Japan is turning into an experience that is both instructive and life changing in very positive ways. It's so good that you have eyes to see! I think I understand very well what you're doing there. It's just the nature of man that someone of your age should attempt to satisfy your curiosity about the world around you by venturing out to look at it. These are some of the things that will steer your later courses, whatever they may be.

You spoke of feelings of euphoria for life. I do know what you mean. I vividly remember the first time this happened to me. I can see it as clearly as if it were yesterday. I was your age – cycling through France, on a long straight secondary road line with tall trees. The sun was shining, there were a few white puffing clouds, the odd farmhouse scattered around, when suddenly I just rolled into a grassy ditch and lay on my back looking up at the sky, unable or unwilling to move. For several minutes I had this amazing euphoric sense of being one with the universe. It was like a revelation the Zen followers strive for and tell us that to achieve this euphoria, we must be able to see and be open to the experience. Doesn't sound like much I'm sure, but for me it was profound.

The business of money is such a huge subject I can't even begin to broach it. One thing is clear and that is – you've got to have some. How much is another question! And what must you do for it! When it became clear to me that to continue practicing law was nothing more than to accumulate money, it made the decision to pursue a path that involved happiness very easy. Not everyone has choices, however and I feel sorry for people when I hear them say how much they hate what they're doing. It usually means they had no choices.

I'm having a visit with Ann Margaret and Larry at the moment. They're on their way to Edmonton from the Dominican Republic where they've had a couple of weeks of sun and surfing. They look so well with their suntans and white teeth. They really are very dear. A short visit – overnight in fact. They're off at the bookstores at the moment. Ann Margaret is a voracious reader.

I phoned Brownie and Betty last week to do my weekly investigation, and although Betty's ankle is mending, Brownie's breathing problem is still there. It's very worrisome. I think that when they did the heart by-pass the surgeon severed the nerve which services the diaphragm. According to the specialist in South Carolina, it would take a very lengthy and complex operation to fix this and he's reluctant to do this so soon after the last operation.

My favorite item on the news lately involved a health spa in the U.S. which used the slogan: "When the aliens land, they're going to eat the fat ones first!" Apparently this outraged all the 'Fat People's Clubs' of America. This afternoon I'm

going to read to a friend who's very ill with cancer and has
been for some time and from there to a vicious bridge game.

Meanwhile, I'm enclosing a bit of Sanskrit for your
edification. The piece is probably 2,580 years old and has
been an inspiration for me for years. Whenever I lose my
focus, this piece helps bring things back to reality.

Look to this day,
For it s is Life,
the very life of Life.
In its brief course lie all the truths and
realities of existence;
the splendor of action,
the glory of power.
For yesterday is but a memory,
and tomorrow only a dream;
but this day,
well lived,
makes every yesterday a memory of happiness
and every tomorrow a vision of hope.
Look well, therefore, to this Day.

I think of you daily and wish you a happy day!

- David

APPRECIATIONS

———⚔———

DAVID
THROUGH THE YEARS

by Sandra Gwyn

David and I met in Halifax in the early 1950s when we were both in out late teens... possibly at the Waegwaltic Club, down on the northwest Arm. We swam in the North Altantic off a slightly rickety dock; when the water got up to 70 degrees Fahrenheit, the boldest would swim right across the Arm.

David was the most dashing of lifeguards, right out of 'Beach Blanket Bingo.' Blonde, athletic, tanned, flirtatious even then, endowed with a rakish wit that sharpened with the years. In the lingo of the era, we described him as a really good head... but it was much later that I discovered that Virginia Woolf had invented the best description for someone like David. She divided the world into people who were 'life enhancers' and people who were not. And David was definitely one of those who enhanced life around him. Among many other things, he was a man who listened.

The other place to hang out with David was on the Dalhousie campus, in the grungy canteen in the old Men's

Residence, where the mingled smoke from Sweet Caps and Craven A cork tips was heavy in the air. He was the centre of a bunch of us – vaguely Bohemian types, we thought ourselves – who met for an hour or so every morning before it was time to saunter off to C.L. Bennett's memorable English 9 history room, where we'd act out the plays we were studying – everything from 'Oedipus Rex' to 'Streetcar Named Desire' – pretty racy for Halifax in the fifties.

David was also at the leading edge of the Glee and Dramatic Society, a ginger group in the midst of transforming a pretty staid organization that went from an annual G & S and an annual Shakespeare into a nervy little gang that put on up-to-the-moment revues. One I recall, titled 'TV or not TV,' was inspired by the fact that later that year – it was 1954 – the first CBC TV station was going to open up in Halifax.

David wrote some of those skits and acted in some of them, but I remember him best as a marvelous dancer. An old yearbook shows him in white shirt and black trousers literally waltzing off the pages in 'Dancing in the Dark' with campus golden girl Nancy Lane.

Remember – this was still the 1950s and actors weren't serious – so David entered Dalhousie Law School and practiced with the prestigious Halifax firm of Kitz & Matheson.

Then, in 1963, along came the Neptune Theatre, the institution that changed his life. Neil Simon's comedies were David's greatest success. (I've heard that when Neil Simon came up to see him in one of his plays, he said, "if David Brown had opened in New York in that play, he'd have been a star!")

Inevitably, the day came, somewhere around 1970, when David decided to give up the law and, as he put it, "run away with the gypsies." David launched a new career as an actor, director and coach in Toronto, Lindsay, North Hatley, Victoria, Stratford and other points east and west.

During those years, we were living in different cities – sometimes in different countries – and our paths rarely crossed. But in 1992, when we moved to Toronto, I discovered that David was a friend for all seasons, the kind you quickly pick up with wherever you'd left off. Then, about four years ago, I discovered, most importantly, that David was a friend for all reasons – a friend who was always there for you. I was very ill and David moved in for a few days. He filled the place with the delicious odor of mustard pickles made according to his mother's recipe. He also got me seriously addicted to 'Jeopardy.'

David left us too young and too soon. Yet he enhanced all of our lives, just as he lit up the stage at Dalhousie so long ago. And he will continue to do so, from here to eternity – for love is stronger than death.

– July 23, 1999

(Sandra Gwyn died of cancer on May 26, 2000)

HE LEFT THE LAW
TO RUN AWAY WITH THE
GYPSIES

by David Hilton

D avid was a man of many parts: a lawyer, an actor and a bridge player among other things. But he is last remembered as an extraordinarily generous friend.

David entered Dalhousie University and divided his time between his law studies and his love of dance and theatre. On graduation he joined the firm of Kitz & Matheson, later to become Kitz, Matheson & Brown, was quickly made partner and carved out a reputation as a litigator and defender in criminal courts. He was a good lawyer and, like many good lawyers, had a sense of theatre.

Once, a group of sailors arrived unannounced at his offices. They were stranded and their ship's foreign owners had not paid their wages. David remembered that you could seize a foreign vessel by nailing a writ to its mast. Armed with the necessary paper and a hammer, he marched down to the Halifax docks with his aggrieved clients. The dramatic gesture was momentarily foiled when he discovered that the mast was made of steel. He returned with Scotch tape.

In 1963, the Neptune Theatre opened in Halifax and David joined the Company. He divided his time between the law and the stage until 1968, when he moved to Toronto. And for almost 20 years thereafter he worked as an actor from Newfoundland to Vancouver Island.

His forte was getting audiences to laugh. Critic Nathan Cohen once referred to him as "one of the best performers of light comedy in the country."

Whether it was in Neil Simon or Sondheim or as a memorable Luther Billis in 'South Pacific,' 'Brownie' delighted audiences. He was particularly attached to Noël Coward's work and gave more than 200 performances in the revue 'Oh Coward,' which toured Canada and the United States.

He once said the secret of playing song-and-dance roles was always to keep moving: "It's tougher for an audience, when they don't like you, to hit you with anything."

His range was wider than many thought. For many years he starred in a number of productions of 'Dracula' and played the lead in 'Doctor Frankenstein's Creature' at Theatre New Brunswick. He completed the 'Grand Guignol' triple by appearing in 'Dr. Jekyll and Mr. Hyde.'

'Brownie' once remarked that he thought Noel Coward's epitaph for himself – that he had a talent to amuse – was an admirable way to describe a life well lived. David also had a talent to amuse, but he had much more. He was so many people's best friend, the one who never let you down.

From 1986 to 1989 he was a member of the Stratford Festival Company. Each season he moved into an apartment in the Stratford home of close friend and actress Roberta Maxwell, and revelled in playing character roles and bridge.

In recent years, Brownie devoted himself to coaching other actors and passing on his knowledge to many colleagues he had worked with on the stage or in film or radio.

(David Hilton was a classmate of David Brown's at Dalhousie Law School ('59))

DAVID THE ACTOR

by Vern Chapman

He was the nicest Dracula you could ever hope to meet. "I never knew anyone who disliked him," said Joyce Gordon about David Edward Brown, not Dracula.

It is a sentiment shared by all of his friends who will miss him profoundly – not only as a delightful human being, but also as one of Canada's most versatile performers.

David's career as a professional actor spanned three decades, but he cut his theatrical teeth in the amateur theatre of Halifax and at Dalhousie University. While in his teens he studied modern dance and classical ballet which, when combined with his enormous talent as an actor and singer, made him a truly triple-threat man.

At Dalhousie, he joined the Glee and Dramatic Society and, according to the local critic, "he nearly stole the show" as Dr. Einstein in their production of 'Arsenic and Old Lace.' He became a member of the Halifax Theatre Ballet Company and, in a college revue called 'Singing on the Seine,' he and his partner electrified the audience with their interpretation of the Apache dance.

After graduating with both a Bachelor of Arts and Bachelor of Law degrees, he joined a Halifax legal firm. But he continued to perform in amateur theatre, playing in such productions for the Halifax Theatre Arts Guild as 'The Reluctant Debutante' and 'The Lady's Not For Burning.'

David made his inaugural debut as a professional actor in 'Romanov and Juliet' during the Neptune Theatre's first season and later as the juvenile lead in 'The Boy Friend.' After six years of dealing with wills, torts and codicils, he took a two-year leave of absence from the legal profession, which stretched, into a lifetime.

He moved to Toronto and from then on, the rest of the country was able to enjoy the awesome talent of this extremely versatile performer. He quickly found his way into TV, films, and radio. He acted, sang and danced on stages from Halifax to Victoria – playing major roles in such diverse shows as 'The Fourposter,' 'A Thousand Clowns,' 'Chaper II,' 'Sleuth,' 'I'll Be Back Before Midnight,' 'California Suite,' 'The Rivals,' 'Who's Afraid of Virgina Woolf?,' 'Hay Fever,' 'Deathtrap,' and 'South Pacific' in which as Luther Billis, clad in a grass skirt and coconut brassiere, he delighted the audience with his hula dancing. 'Oh Coward' became one of his greatest triumphs, with performances in Ottawa, Toronto, Chicago and Boston. From 1986 to 1989, he added to his laurels as a member of the Stratford Festival Company.

His versatility is exemplified in a biographical note in the Neptune Theatre program for 'The Apple Cart.' It reads: "In the past fourteen months, Mr. Brown has played a greedy, conniving homosexual killer, a middle class London antique dealer, a concerned parent, a frustrated and near demented tennis player, an evil New England auctioneer, a dancing/singing vitamin pill, a crazed TV game show host, a sore-footed podiatrist, an absent-minded professor, a cockney pub owner, an upper-class English philanderer, an optimistically bankrupt businessman, an aristocratic British diplomat, and three of the seven dwarfs!

LAUGHTER
SURROUNDED HIM
DAVID IN HALIFAX

by David Renton

In February of 1964, the furnace in my rented cottage at Purcell's Cove exploded, covering all of my possessions in a film of oil and soot and leaving me without heat. David Brown took me in. He had a spacious apartment on Victoria Road; and at the time we were both performing in 'Diary of a Scoundrel.' David embraced the come-from-aways like myself, Ted and Dawn Follows, George Sperdakos and especially Mary MacMurray, with great generosity and loving friendship.

For a year and a half, during our late 'salad days,' we were roommates. We worked hard and played even harder. David had a Sprite sports car and when the summer came we sped off, top down, to Hubbard's, Schooner Cove, Portuguese Cove, Duncan's Cove…to Taby's, Don Oliver's, Matheson's, Kitz's, Pigot's, and a host of other good friends and colleagues.

David's wit and agile mind kept those around him in a

state of constant amusement and good spirits. He did so many things so very well – he entertained on many levels, he was a fine cook and host and he inspired me to make exotic paellas and Pat Harris' never-fail cheesecake. We steamed fresh plump scallops in Chablis, marinated and made sauces with Châteauneuf-du-Pape and consumed crates of the then affordable South African wines. In the midst of this entertaining, David told wonderful stories. He was always able to see the comic element in any situation. Laughter surrounded him.

David was a gifted performer. I had the good fortune to act with him in 'Romanoff and Juliet,' 'John A. Beats the Devil,' 'Come Blow Your Horn,' 'The Crucible,' 'Arsenic and Old Lace,' 'Henry IV, Part One,' 'The Wooden World,' 'The Taming of the Shrew,' and 'Ondine.'

In the spring of 1978, I directed David and Joan Gregson in 'Same Time Next Year.' On opening night, the Brown family cheering section sat in the front row of the balcony. They, along with the rest of the audience, were swept away by David's skillful comedy and moved by his emotional power as his character spoke of the loss of his son in Vietnam. David and Joan played to sold-out houses during the run of the show, a tour of the province and for three additional weeks.

David was a good friend to me. Through him I met my wife, with whom David had danced in musicals, the Halifax Theatre Ballet Company and with Don Warner's band. He was a true gentleman and I am proud to have had him as a friend.

Have a grand slam on cloud nine, old friend.

- August 4, 1999

DAVID,
MY PARTNER

by Anna MacCormack Geddes

Memories of David spring to mind when I hear the song 'Under Paris Skies.' I recall David and I dancing as partners in our first venture into choreography – I believe the Revue was called 'Singing in the Seine' – and celebrating when one of our 'finales' (his suggestion) seemed to defy gravity, much to our delight.

Over the years we acted together on CBC Radio. My fondest memories are of a daily serial we did together in 1960. David and I had two of the leading roles in a serial called 'Edge of Tomorrow'…we had tremendous fun and it went trans-Canada!

When David and I were in each other's company, we always brought out each other's sense of humour. Is it any wonder when I think of David I think of the best fun I've had in my life? We had a sort of brother/sister attitude toward each other, knowing so many of each other's relatives and friends. But the fun came also from the genuine affection and respect we had for each other. We enjoyed each other's successes and were ready to do whatever we could to bolster them.

David made me feel as if my company was a k
to him – that was his gift to me. David allowed othei
to feel lovable by taking an authentic delight in their com
His generosity of spirit was, I believe, boundless. His lov
life such that one couldn't imagine it over – and of course
isn't. Thank God for Eternity.